*Joakim offers a necessary toolbox and important perspectives for everyone who wants to have a positive impact on the world.*
**Jan Artem Henriksson,** *Executive Director*
*Inner Development Goals, Senior Fellow*
*at Human Flourishing Network at Harvard*

*Joakim Eriksson has created a strong framework for understanding the intrinsic connections between body, mind, and leadership. Packed with insights for how to strengthen leaders' inner capabilities, the framework provides actionable advice for building a more effective and sustainable leadership practice.*
**Anders Møller Jakobsen,** *Deputy Director General,*
*City of Copenhagen*

*This book resonates deeply with my own leadership journey. With a background in both the military and logistics, I appreciate Eriksson's practical approach, seamlessly blending real-world wisdom with neuroscience and psychology. A must-read for leaders like me who thrive on challenges in life.*
**Patrik Strid,** *Vice President Operations DFDS*

*This is foundational for great leaders. The understanding of looking inside yourself and exercising the brain has changed the way we look at training and is now foundational for our leadership programs. Thank you, Joakim, for bringing this to our organisation!*
**Monica Bolander,** *Learning &*
*Development Director, EQT Group*

# Building Sustainable Leadership from the Inside

Drawing on contemporary neuroscience, this book shows leaders how they can literally train their mind to become more resilient and have a more sustainable impact.

This is a research-backed and practical guide for how to grow inner capabilities enabling sustainable leadership in this time. It is built around five areas that many leaders will recognise as being challenging on a personal level, such as how to stay calm under pressure, navigate in uncertainty or collaborate skilfully with people with diverse points of views. While many leadership books describe the importance of such traits, few show how to actually cultivate them. Grounded in multiple fields of research, this book offers a practical training manual for the mind. With more than 40 reflections and exercises, it offers a guided tour to an 'inner gym', showing readers how to cultivate these capabilities.

Leaders who have realised that it takes more than IQ and theoretical knowledge to create sustainable impact and are looking for ways to deepen their leadership capacity and authenticity will find them in this practical training manual for the mind.

**Joakim Eriksson** is an experienced leader, facilitator and executive coach with over 30 years of experience with leadership and organisational development. He works with multinational organisations and draws on research and practices from a wide variety of fields such as neuroscience, systems thinking, contemplative traditions as well as his own leadership experience. Joakim lives with his family in the south of Sweden.

For more information, visit www.IQL-Institute.com.

# Building Sustainable Leadership from the Inside

## How to Grow the Inner Capabilities We Need to Lead

Joakim Eriksson

Routledge
Taylor & Francis Group

NEW YORK AND LONDON

Designed cover image: Nicolai Aarup Larsen

First published 2025
by Routledge
605 Third Avenue, New York, NY 10158

and by Routledge
4 Park Square, Milton Park, Abingdon, Oxon, OX14 4RN

*Routledge is an imprint of the Taylor & Francis Group, an informa business*

© 2025 Joakim Eriksson

ISBN: 9781032778624 (hbk)
ISBN: 9781032759821 (pbk)
ISBN: 9781003485148 (ebk)

DOI: 10.4324/9781003485148

Typeset in Sabon
by codeMantra

To all the brave and dedicated people
who are willing to work with themselves
to make a positive difference in the world

# Contents

# Introduction

In business schools and universities, we learn ways to analyse, organise and manage the world around us, but seldom how to manage ourselves. Yet, our inner, personal qualities such as presence, focus, self-awareness and empathy have a great influence on how we show up in the world. And if we are in some kind of leadership position, how we show up will surely have an influence on people around us and our organisation.

Personal development can be seen as something self-oriented, but I will invite you to think of it the other way around. Working seriously with our own inner development can make us live more fulfilling lives, but also become better agents for positive change, no matter if the topic is sustainability, inclusion of any other important and complex issue.

The world around us is constantly changing, so how can we as leaders and human beings adapt and grow to meet the challenges of modern work life? According to contemporary research in neuroscience and psychology, all of us can train our inner capabilities to cope more skilfully with uncertainty, distractions, polarisation, etc., as well as increase our awareness about our own biases and habitual behaviors. By engaging in our own development, we can literally change our brain and how we show up in the world. The intention of this book is to give you a practical introduction to how.

The book is built around five themes, each related to situations and challenges that many of us, especially in leadership positions, can relate to:

- How to be sustainable over time in a high-pressure work environment.
- How to stay smart under pressure and show up as the version of ourselves we would like to be, even in difficult situations.
- How to be with the discomforts of change, complexity and uncertainty, without becoming reactive or going into a rigid self-protection mode.
- How to collaborate and co-create with people who have different agendas and points of view than us.
- How to build personal resilience, find our inner compass and stay connected to the bigger picture.

DOI: 10.4324/9781003485148-1

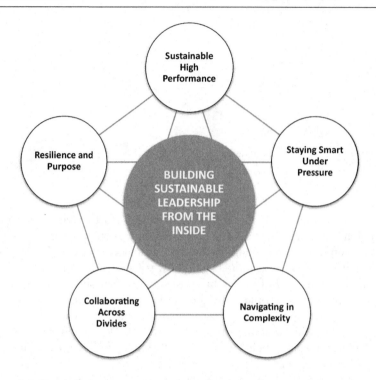

*Figure 0.1* The five elements of building sustainable leadership from the inside.

For each of the chapters, we will unpack typical challenges that you probably can relate to. We will then explore what contemporary research and thought leaders from different fields can tell us about how to handle these challenges, and most importantly, we will translate the science into practical exercises and routines you can integrate into your own life.

Writing this book, I am standing on the shoulders of many giants in fields such as systems thinking, contemplative practices, neuroscience, psychology and leadership. You will get an introduction to many different theories, principles and practices, each of them worthy of deeper exploration. If some of the areas feel especially relevant for you, I have made sure to point you to sources where you can explore things beyond the practices we work with here. You can see the book as a concentrated bouillon cube of tips for working with inner development, or a handful of seeds of inspiration that can be planted and cultivated.

Of the various elements we cover, I would not claim to have invented much that is new in and by itself. What I see as my contribution, however, is connecting dots, bringing together, and making synthesis of research, theories, and practices from a wide variety of fields. Although it is not my aspiration to write an academic book, I have therefore chosen to refer to many of my sources so you can easily go deeper into any area that gets your attention.

Instead of filling pages with a lot of case stories, I have tried to write as straight forward as possible, introducing practical tools and exercises applicable in the daily life of leaders. The invitation is for you to try things out yourself and discover your own case stories.

The good news is that what we cover in this book are trainable skills. There is plenty of research indicating that doing the different practices can have very positive effects on your capability to cope with common challenges. The bad news is that what we cover are trainable skills... That's right, just reading the book may inspire you, but won't really lead to any sustainable changes.

See this book as a guided tour to an inner gym. If you ever signed up for a gym membership, you might have got a guided tour by a personal trainer who showed you different exercises to strengthen different parts of your body. In the same way, this book will introduce you to a wide variety of research-backed practices that can strengthen your inner capabilities. As with a physical gym, to get the effects, you will have to do the practices. To support you, there are also guided audio practices accompanying the different chapters. You can search for *Meditations for Leaders (Joakim Eriksson)* to find them on your preferred audio platform.

This book is the practice manual I wish I would have had access to earlier in my leadership career. I am not sharing anything I haven't used and practiced myself over an extended time. I have worked with thousands of leaders on these topics, but this doesn't mean everything will be relevant to your unique needs. You will sense what practices would be relevant and useful for you. My aspiration is to make you curious enough to try things out for yourself and make your own experiences.

May your exploration be of benefit both for you and the people you touch in your daily life.

## A short backstory

This book is not about me, but about some of the experiences and learnings I have collected along the way, and that might be helpful for you as well. Just to give some context, I want to give a short introduction to the different areas from which I will draw on knowledge and experience.

My first real encounter with organisational life and leadership was in the military in my early 20s. I did my service at a ranger regiment and trained to lead a small group of divers to do infiltration and recognizance missions. Although I hope I will never use the military skills I acquired, that period of my life taught me some important lessons about self-leadership and team collaboration. I learned that we can push our boundaries much more than we think as long as we are motivated, but I also learned the importance of knowing what our limitations and weaknesses are, so we don't get surprised by them. I experienced what it means to have deep trust in your teammates. Not that you must love each other, but just knowing that they will be there for you when you hit your limit and need help makes a big difference. Maybe surprisingly to some, one of my key learnings from the military was that admitting vulnerability makes you strong as a team.

When I was in my early 30s, I had progressed through a slow but steady career at one of Scandinavia's largest tour operators and was promoted to my first C-level position. My ego was quite flattered by that, but I probably should have declined. I was not yet mature for that position and soon found myself in deep water. I was struggling to fill out my new role, and at the same time, I became a father for the first time.

What played out was a small, but real, life crisis, where I had to recalibrate how to run my life. The benefit of this little crisis was that I couldn't solve it by keeping on doing what had brought me success earlier in life; putting my head down and grinding on. I had to stop, reflect, and turn my attention inward to regain my footing. This was the starting point for my interest in the topics we will cover in this book.

Another important experience I gathered during this period was from the dynamics of being a part of a senior management team. As an organisation, we were in the midst of a transition from an analog business model to a new way of working where the internet changed the rules of the game. In the process, we had to evaluate, decide and execute on a number of major changes in our organisation.

Here I started noticing an interesting pattern. After evaluating different options, we as a management team would conclude and decide on the best way forward. But, although we had all agreed on a decision, we didn't always carry out what we had decided to do. Consciously or subconsciously, we sometimes resisted the consequences of our own decisions, and held on to old behaviors. This experience sparked my interest in trying to understand what is happening in people and organisations, beyond and below the conscious, rational processes.

In my 40s, I had made a shift from the hospitality industry to management consulting. With organisational and leadership development as my main focus areas, I was facilitating strategy processes, coaching leaders, and heading various leadership development programs for larger organisations. In this context, another important insight started to dawn on me. At the start of a development program, we usually asked participants what they wanted to get out of it. At the top of the list was often 'to learn more tools…'. But although we shared similar theory, models and techniques with our participants, there were enormous differences in how they were able to apply and practice the 'tools' they had learned. I started to understand that there is a big difference between what your head knows, what your heart believes in and what your hands can actually do. Just having a box full of tools, doesn't make you a good carpenter.

I started to realise that just sharing intellectual 'tools' with participants would not help them develop skillful behaviors. To have real impact, people 'holding the tools' must also learn to develop themselves. This is when I decided to dedicate my consulting career to exploring how we can develop our inner skills and qualities so we can use our knowledge effectively and wisely.

For 15 years, I have explored personal development and leadership from many different perspectives, ranging from martial arts practice and meditation to neuroscience and developmental psychology. Although I have been rather diligent in my exploration, I do not want to position myself as the expert in any of these areas. My contribution is rather to make useful synthesis between different domains, and package it in a way that can be easily accessible and practical. My hope is that this will inspire you to do your own exploration.

## The business case for exploring the inner aspects of leadership

Most of us would like to think of ourselves as very rational beings. The more educated we are, the more we might subscribe to that idea. In 2002, Daniel Kahneman won the Nobel Prize in economics based on his work on human decision-making. Kahneman is a behavioral psychologist and brought new perspectives to why organisations and markets work the way they do.

In his book *Thinking Fast and Slow*, Kahneman[1] describes humans as guided by what he calls Systems 1 and 2. System 1 is the fast, intuitive part of our mind that quickly recognises patterns and draws conclusions, unfortunately often based on biases rather than on facts. System 2 is the part of our mind that is analytical and rational, but unfortunately also rather slow.

A key message from Kahneman's research is that most of our decision-making seems to be driven from System 1, i.e. we are often subconsciously ruled by our assumptions and ingrained thinking patterns. If we hold this to be true (it can be difficult to argue with Nobel Prize Laureates), it has interesting implications for how we act and lead.

In large parts of our daily life, System 1 will probably serve us well. When we, for example, face a familiar situation, it is often useful to apply previously tested solutions and methods. Hence, System 1 can help us by quickly serving up ideas that have worked before.

However, when we are facing new or complex situations for which we cannot rely on previous experience to guide us, System 1 can lead us astray by drawing conclusions based on biases or skewing data to fit into an outdated narrative. Working with the more complex and adaptive challenges in life requires us to turn off our mental autopilots and observe all the dynamics in the system we are part of. This is the work of System 2, our reflecting and analytical mind.

Both systems have their benefits, but to lead well and act skilfully, we must learn to recognise and leverage their different characteristics. When facing new and complex situations in our life, it is crucial to be able to pause our habitual thinking and autopilot behaviors long enough to make more conscious decisions. One of the purposes of this book is to explore practical ways to do this.

## How stressors affect our cognitive functioning

Our nervous system has developed over thousands of generations and is optimised for survival. We should keep in mind, however, that more than 90% of these generations have lived on the savannah. Most of our neurological hard wiring is designed for a very different lifestyle than we have today, which can cause some challenges if we don't pay attention to it.

A part of our hard wiring is our so-called autonomous nervous system which can be divided into the sympathetic and parasympathetic nervous system.

The sympathetic nervous system (SNS), also called our fight or flight system, is what gets activated when we perceive something as threatening. Our heart rate and blood pressure go up, adrenalin and cortisol go out in our body. We are ready for action.

The parasympathetic nervous system (PNS), is our recovery system. When that activates, heart rates and blood pressure go down, we feel calmer, and healing, digestion, etc., start in our body.

Evolution has developed both these systems as important functions for our survival. If we ran into something dangerous, we could react quickly. When danger was over, we could heal and recover again. In today's work environment, we meet few physical threats, but SNS instead gets activated by an angry e-mail from a client, a fast-approaching deadline or declining sales numbers. The physical reaction in our body from these perceived 'threats' are the same as when we encountered a dangerous animal on the savannah.

Getting a stress reaction is not negative per se. It can help us be alert and ready to act. What can be problematic to our well-being is if we spend too much time with the SNS activated. This system was designed to activate only when we encountered an immediate threat. Nowadays, many professionals in high-pressure environments spend most of their time with a low to medium activation of the SNS. This is not what we have been designed for and can have long-term consequences for our health.

Another important aspect, is the way SNS activation influences our cognitive functioning. When our fight or flight system activates, we go into protection mode. The consequences are that we tend to become more:

- Oriented around our own needs
- Short sighted
- Tunnel visioned
- Likely to repeat old behavioral patterns

From a survival point of view, this makes sense. When facing an immediate danger, it probably didn't pay off to sit down and hold hands, discuss, and try to reach consensus with a lot of other people. It probably worked better to fight or run to the tree that had saved you before, and to focus on protecting yourself and the ones most important to you.

Due to how we are evolutionarily wired, it seems to be very difficult for us to be adaptive, creative and altruistic when we are in self-protection mode. Despite our sophistication as human beings, the more primitive survival functions of our brain can kick in even in a management team that is under pressure. Also experienced leaders can struggle to take in new data and see the bigger picture when they get stressed. Instead of stepping out of our autopilot thinking and trying to take a new perspective on a situation, when stressed we tend to push harder, clinging to methods that have worked for us before.

On the contrary, what happens when we manage to step out of the sympathetic mode? When we feel safe, relaxed or inspired, we get more easy access to the parts of our brain related to:

- Big picture thinking
- Ability to relate to the needs of others
- Openness for new ideas and perspectives

When we feel safe and calm, it is easier for us to think strategically, collaborate with others and be creative. That is just how we are hard wired.

This leads to a relevant question for all of us working in organisations: What neural mode is most helpful to be in, in which situation? Clearly, different modes are useful in different contexts.

Sympathetic activation enables us to react quickly when immediate action is needed and to be very focused when an important deadline is approaching. Parasympathetic activation through relaxation or the experience of positive emotions can enable us to be more creative, open to other people's points of view, see a problem from a new perspective, etc.

Experience shows that many of us spend an unproportionally large part of our working hours with low to medium levels of activation of our stress response system, likely blocking us from showing up fully as the open-minded, collaborative and co-creative professionals most of us would like to be.

One of the objectives of this book is to help you reflect more on which version of yourself shows up in different situations in life. Building on that, we will explore a wide variety of techniques for deliberately shifting to a mind state that helps you navigate difficult situations more skilfully.

Learning these skills can make us more capable of tackling complex problems as well as everyday challenges. When we deliberately can switch off our mental autopilots and step out of our self-protection mode, we can be of more benefit to those around us and to the world at large.

## Reflection, practice and the idea of mental training

We live in a society where intellectual knowledge is highly valued but think a moment about all the things you know <u>about</u>, but not how to <u>do</u>. We like to learn about new 'tools', but sometimes forget that the person holding the tool must <u>practice</u> to get skilled at using it.

In this book, we are going to cover personal 'tools' for coping with various situations. These tools are focused on the inner aspects of leadership, for example, how to stay focused, regulate emotions or evoke compassion. I will give enough of a scientific background and conceptional understanding for you to get the idea, but most of all I will invite you to practice and explore things for yourself.

Thanks to what is known as neuroplasticity, our brains adapt and grow with training, just like our physical muscles. This opens for the fantastic possibility to actually train our brains to better cope with the challenges of life. We might have thought that our brain is developed and ready by the time we get to our 20s, but findings in neuroscience and psychology point to that it can, and should, keep developing throughout our life.

Given how much the environment we work in, and the expectations being put on us, changes throughout our lives (remember what work was like before smart phones and virtual meetings…), we are lucky that our brains can adapt. Although our brains naturally adapt to circumstances, we can also accelerate this process with dedicated practices. The content of this book is designed around exactly that, to help you strengthen a set of mental 'muscles' that might be useful in today's reality and especially in leadership roles.

The way we go to the 'gym' in this book is to work with reflections and various mental exercises, for example, visualisations and meditations. Frequently throughout the text, there will be icons like these on the side, indicating a practice. The head icon indicates a reflection exercise to help you relate to and integrate the content we cover. The dumbbell icon indicates a mental exercise intended to be done on a regular basis to build familiarity and skill. You can think of each of these practices as small fitness exercises for your brain. The more you do them, the bigger change you will notice over time.

Do not expect any quick fixes, however. Although you may get some immediate aha-moments and positive effects from some of the practices, developing our mental capabilities is more like gardening than engineering. It takes some time and patience to gradually grow new capabilities. I invite you to find the areas that are of special interest for you, select a few practices and do them with regularity.

I will refer a lot to research and science throughout the book to give you a sense of where the ideas, principles and practices stem from. Everything I share is consistent with existing research, but not restricted to what can be scientifically measured with today's methods. When it comes to the inner aspects of us as human beings, there are many things we can experience clearly without science necessarily having the tools to quantify it.

As a neuroscientist said when I attended a training on emotional intelligence many years ago; "Take my research as inspiration, and then go and try things out in your own research laboratory – your own life".

As you will see as you go through the book, the different chapters are interlinked. There are benefits to reading the chapters in the order they are presented, but you can also jump around and explore the topics that have the most interest for you.

Good luck with your practice.

## Note

1 *Thinking Fast and Slow* (2011) is probably Kahneman's most well-known book. You can see him addressing key points from this work in a keynote at Google. Search for: *Thinking, Fast and Slow – Daniel Kahneman – Talks at Google*. His recent book *Noice: A Flaw in Human Judgement* (2021) also explores the human mind in relation to decision-making. Go to kahneman.scholar.princeton.edu/publications if you want to learn more about Kahneman's work and publications.

# Chapter 1

# Sustainable high performance

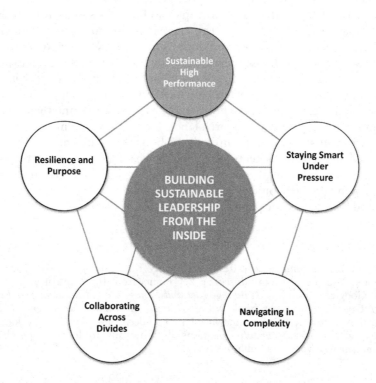

*Figure 1.1* The five areas of building sustainable leadership from the inside.

**Overview Chapter 1: Sustainable high performance**

In this first part of the book, we leverage the last decades of neuro-scientific research to better understand how our brain and nervous system react to the common stressors of modern work life.

DOI: 10.4324/9781003485148-2

Building on this research, we explore various techniques that can help us work in synch with our brain, and train our ability to stay calm and focused in a world full of distractions.

*These are some of the areas we are going to cover:*

- Exploring the difference between positive and negative stress.
- The business case for working with micro-recovery for sustainable high performance.
- How multitasking effects our cognitive functioning.
- The idea of 'meshing' – discerning what we focus our energy on.
- Attention training – improving our ability to be present and focused.
- Introduction to the mechanics of mindfulness training.
- Resetting to calm – practical techniques for soothing our nervous system.
- The power of the pause – building micro-pauses into our workdays to perform better.
- The wise use of self-compassion.
- Creating a culture that supports sustainable high performance.

*How this chapter links to and supports other part of the book:*

- Learning to manage our energy lays a foundation for the chapter on *Resilience*.
- The foundational practices of sharpening our focus and attention introduced in this chapter are also key for the elements of self-awareness and self-leadership we will cover in *Staying Smart Under Pressure*.
- The ability to 'reset to calm' during stressful times enhances our emotional regulation, which supports both *Navigating in Complexity* as well as *Collaborating across Divides*.

*Supporting audio material:*

- There are guided audio practices accompanying this chapter. Search for *Meditations for Leaders* (*Joakim Eriksson*) to find them on your preferred audio platform.

## Working in an always-on reality

Having worked in corporate environments for over 30 years, I cannot help but see that workloads and potential stressors tend to increase with the scope of responsibility. As leaders, we are expected to relate to and cope with a wide array of topics, and we can experience we never get the time to attend to everything we would like to.

I can clearly remember a moment when I was in my twenties and had been working as a first-line manager for two years. I was hurrying between meetings, and suddenly, sitting in my car at a red light, the insight struck me; I will never again be finished.... My to-do list will never be fully ticked off. I will never leave work feeling that all tasks are completed.

In a way, this was an overwhelming thought, but at the same time, I relaxed. I realised that being a leader was not so much about completing tasks and ticking boxes, but to navigate skilfully in a never-ending stream of demands and be conscious about how to prioritise my time.

Unfortunately, this insight did not make everything clear and easy. Throughout my career, I have still struggled to 'be enough', prioritise my time and balance my workload. What I learned, though, was that there is seldom anyone else who filters how many things will come our way. We will have to find our own way to stay sustainable over time.

Over the last decades, I have seen a continuous stream of new methods and technology introduced to help us handle our work, be more effective and save us time. I have myself happily been using time managers, palm pilots, smart phones, etc. But to be honest – do we ever find ourselves with more time on our hands? Do you remember when e-mail was first introduced? It was supposed to save us so much time now that we didn't have to send fax messages. Where did that end up? What will be the next technology that will 'save us time'?

My point here is that when used in a skillful way, technology can offer us a lot of help. But technology alone will not help us live and work in a sustainable way. To live well and thrive in a high-pressure work environment, we will also have to develop inner technologies (focus, emotional intelligence, making conscious priorities, etc.) so we can cope with the reality created by the outer technologies.

Stress and demands are an inevitable part of life, but we can learn to get better at surfing the waves. In the next chapters, we will explore different perspectives and techniques that can help you relate to and navigate stress and workloads more skilfully. Some of them may seem like common sense and some maybe more thought provoking. I invite you to explore what could be useful in your work life.

## Understanding the difference between positive and negative stress

Many of us would see stress as something to be avoided, but it is worth remembering that stress is an evolutionary response, hard wired into our brain and body – and it is there to keep us safe. One of the neuroscientists

I have been studying with, Dr. Rick Hanson, has this comical but helpful explanation:

*Our ancestors were nervous monkeys. Because the chill monkeys all got eaten...*

The point is that evolution has rewarded individuals that detected dangers early and had apt stress responses, helping them to survive. Next time we feel stressed, we can try to smile and thank evolution for this built-in survival tool.

Fast forward to today's work environment, we don't meet many physical dangers in our offices, but our stress responses instead get triggered by social interactions, feelings of not meeting expectations, etc. Actually, one of the definitions for stress is when we feel that 'demands exceed our resources to cope'. The interesting thing here is that, unlike when we are hunted by dangerous animals, the stress most of us experience today is created by the stories we are telling ourselves about the situations we are in.

Professor Modupe Akinola at Colombia University Business School has been researching stress in high-performing professionals and makes a point that our narrative will influence how we stress.[1] Her research shows that not all stress is negative. The raised heart rate, adrenalin and cortisol can actually make us perform better at crucial moments – we can feel alert and ready to act. When we face a challenge that feels positively exciting and challenging for us, we can get a dopamine release that feels good.

However, Akinola has also found that stress can work as a disabling factor when we have a negative narrative around the situation at hand. In these situations, our physiological reaction is based on fear, rather than the possibilities the situation offers.

One of the practices Akinola recommends when she coaches high-performing leaders is to reflect on the stories we are telling ourselves around the situations that cause us stress and reframe how we think about them.

Here are some questions to explore for yourself:

- *What are situations that often cause you to feel stress?*
- *In what situations do you experience that your stress actually helps you perform, and when does it become debilitating?*
- *If you look deeper at these situations, what is the narrative you have around it?*
- *Is the story you are telling yourself based on previous experiences?*
- *How do these experiences relate to current conditions?*
- *Are you adding a layer of self-criticism to the situation, and is that helpful?*

To reframe these situations, please reflect on the following:

- *What is it I might fear?*
- *What would be the worst that could happen?*
- *How likely is it that would happen?*
- *What are the possibilities related to this situation?*
- *What is it that I care for?*
- *How can my stress actually help me achieve what is important for me?*

Reframing how we think about a situation can support what Professor Carol Dweck at Stanford University calls a learning or growth mindset,[2] which helps us tackle setbacks and challenges more constructively.

As we started this chapter, stress doesn't have to be negative, but it surely can be. To some degree, it depends on the stories we are telling ourselves. Robert Sapolsky, another professor at Stanford University, has done extensive work on stress and published a book called *Why Zebras Don't Get Ulcers*, where he points to how stress is important for our survival, but also can make us sick.[3]

Dweck, Sapolsky and Akinola all point to how the way we think and relate to the world around us will influence our levels of stress. But a note of caution here. Even with mental reframing and applying a growth mindset, there are still limits to how many things we can take on in a day. In our next section, we will explore the importance of balancing performance with recovery.

## The 50/10 principle

In my early 20s, I did my military service at a ranger regiment. As expected, it was a both physically and mentally demanding experience. Especially during the first couple of months where we all knew that whoever couldn't keep up with the tempo and the challenges would be discharged.

What surprised me, however, was that although the demands were high, we learned from the start the importance of recovery. Whether we were marching, swimming or any other activity, we were taught the principle of going on for 50 minutes, and then taking a 10-minute break, to rest, replenish food/water and adjust our gear, before we continued.

As testosterone pumped, in those days mainly male, soldiers, we were eager to show our instructors that we weren't tired and could keep going without any breaks. But the experienced officers just bluntly replied: "We are not interested in whether you feel strong right now. We are interested how strong and battle ready you are in weeks and months from now, when we have kept going like this".

What I learned then was that endurance depends on making recovery a part of our routine. No matter how tough we think we are, sooner or later we come to a limit where our performance will start to deteriorate.

When it relates to physical training, this is probably rather common sense. Most of us know that if we want to build physical strength, we need to both put a reasonable level of stress on our body by lifting weights or doing cardiovascular workouts, and then also make sure the body gets time to recover between workouts. However, we seem to forget this when it comes to the mental perspectives. We often expect ourselves and others to grind on, without giving our brain a break every now and then. This is probably why we have a pandemic of burnouts in the world.

If we want to perform well over time, we might want to take some inspiration from the 50/10-principles I learned back at the ranger regiment. I invite you to take a moment now to reflect on:

- *What works as physical and mental recovery for you?*
- *Where do you give yourself permission to really relax?*
- *How do you naturally build pauses into your workdays?*
- *What difference do you notice when you 'muddle through' a day, or when you get some breaks along the way?*

A bit later in this book, we will get back to various techniques for building micro-breaks into our work life.

## The effects of multitasking

One way many of us try to keep up with a high in-flow of tasks is to multitask. We might be switching between writing a report, checking messages on our phone and preparing a presentation. Or the classical scenario of sitting in a meeting and using the time to answer a few e-mails. Given that our technology gives us the possibility to engage with multiple tasks at almost any given moment, there are plenty of opportunities here.

Now, let us do a little experiment called 'I am great multitasker'. I first tried this exercise myself many years ago when attending a seminar led by Rasmus Hougaard. Hougaard founded the organisation Potential Project and has written multiple useful books on mind training.[4]

To do the exercise, please find a pen and a blank piece of paper. Your first task is to copy these two lines onto your paper. Use a timer and see how fast you can do it.

**I am a great multitasker**
1 2 3 4 5 6 7 8 9 10 11 12 13 14 15 16 17 18 19 20

Depending on how fast you are at using pen and paper these days, I would guess you used somewhere in between 15 and 30 seconds to write these two lines.

Now, let us try the same exercise again. This time, however, we are going to do what we so often do in our everyday life when we are busy, we are going to multitask. The way we are simulating multitasking here is by writing every other letter/number and shifting between the lines every time. This means starting with writing the letter 'I' on the top line, go down to the second line to write '1', then up to the topline again to write 'a' and so on....

It is the same total amount of letters and numbers to write, you are just going to be more 'effective' by shifting lines between every letter and number. Put your timer on, and good luck...!

-----

What did you notice? How big was the time difference? Did you feel more relaxed or more stressed the second time around?

This little exercise (which I can recommend running with your team if you have a lot of colleagues who believe in the benefits of multitasking) indicates what research has shown; our brains are not very good at multitasking.

Now you might want to protest and argue that you know of many occasions where you can multitask well, and yes – of course, you can. Our brains have evolved to handle multiple things at the same time, but the way it does that is by running most of the activities on autopilot.

Imagine that we learn to drive a car. Shifting gears isn't easy at the start so it requires our full attention. As we get more experienced, however, we can shift gears without using much cognitive attention. Same goes for many other things in life. When certain activities have become automated, we can perform many of them simultaneously without using much mental energy on them.

When we talk about multitasking as a problem, we are referring to trying to do multiple things at the same time that require cognitive capacity or frontal lobe activation. That part of our brain has limited processing capacity and can basically only focus on one thing at the time.

Let us take the scenario that you are in a meeting, and you are listening to a colleague doing a presentation. You just need to answer a few e-mails, so you discreetly open your inbox and start typing away. You might have the illusion that you are actually listening to the presentation at the same time that you are answering e-mails, but what your brain actually does is shifting your attention back and forth between the presenter and your e-mail. The result for your brain is the same as in the exercise we just did. The shifting of attention back and forth requires much more energy for your brain, you are likely to make more mistakes and use more time in total to accomplish your tasks.

Basically, what research indicates is that a good way to make sure we feel overwhelmed, stressed and tired after a day at work is to multitask as much as possible...

Ok, so this is not necessarily happy news for anyone of us. Multitasking is still part of our reality, and depending on our job roles, it can be very difficult to avoid. The game changer here is to become aware of our multitasking habits. Surely, there are many occasions where we will find ourselves in situations where we need to multitask one way or the other. However, by knowing how that influences our brain and our effectiveness, we might want to approach our work differently.

Here are some questions you can reflect on around your own multitasking habits:

- *Would it be possible for you to set periods of time for undisturbed work?*
  *(Some research indicates that we work best when we work in undisturbed bursts of 25 minutes, followed by a short break. Search for 'Pomodoro technique' to read more.)*
- *What notifications do you have activated on your devices?*
  *(Just hearing a notification pulls part of your attention away from what you are doing, even if you don't check your device.)*
- *How can you avoid unnecessarily interrupting each other at work?*
- *What could be helpful ground rules that would help you and your team to use time more effectively?*
  *(By having a shared understanding of how our brain works, we can work with it, rather than against it.)*

Many of us have experienced the sense of 'flow' when we are fully absorbed in what we are doing and time just flies. In these flow states, studied and described by Mihaly Csikszentmihalyi[5] and many others, we are often both stress free and effective. But to get into that state we must create conditions where our mind can really focus. Part of that is creating time and space for undisturbed work, but also cultivating our ability to be present and focused on what we are doing. We will explore this further in later sections on attention training.

## The idea of 'meshing' – choosing what to focus our energy on

As we discussed earlier, a part of an active engagement in work and life can be that we at times experience being overwhelmed by the number of things we need to relate to and act on. Meshing is a term in psychology sometimes used to describe the ability to 'let things pass through', rather than try to control and manage everything. I have found this idea important in my own leadership career, especially when changing positions and taking on larger areas of responsibility.

Let's play with a metaphor for a moment. Imagine that you and a friend are standing in a river with water up to your shoulders. You are trying to hold a sail between you against the flow of the river. How would that feel? Even if the river is flowing slowly, you would feel a lot of pressure on the sail, as it doesn't let any water through.

Now imagine you exchange the sail for a fishing net, the kind with two poles with flags on the top, and a net between the poles. You and your friend grab each of the poles and hold the net out between you as you did with the sail. What is your experience now? You will most likely still feel the movement of the river pushing on the net, but it is less heavy. This is the idea of 'meshing' – not letting everything that happens 'push you' but let more things 'pass through you'.

To stay with the metaphor for a moment, a fishing net doesn't let everything through though. The net lets water and small fish through but catches the bigger fishes. The sort of fish that this particular net was designed for. Applying the idea of meshing doesn't mean you are not caring about things. You are just focusing your attention and energy on the important stuff.

The idea of meshing is related to the tricky but important topic of acceptance. If you fall into the category of people who like to 'fix' things, you might see acceptance as indicating lack of commitment. But acceptance in this context refers to our ability to see things for what they _are_ at this very moment, without wasting emotional energy if things are not the way we would like them to be. An everyday example of this could be getting stuck in a traffic jam or on a delayed train. It is easy to get upset and frustrated, which, of course, does nothing to change or improve the situation.

A part of sustainable high performance is to be selective with what you put your focus and energy on. Especially when we are transitioning into higher leadership positions, there is always a risk that we try to keep track of and manage the same level of details as we did in our previous position. It can therefore be worth reflecting on a regular basis if we are applying 'the right type of net' in our work.

If you at times feel overwhelmed by the number of things you need to handle, feel free to take a moment to reflect on the following questions:

- *What are the situations where you typically feel overwhelmed?*
- *What are the key priorities in your life and in your work?*
- *Are there things you spend (mental) energy on, that have little or no impact on your key priorities?*

- *What could you let 'pass through my net', without any significant consequences?*
- *How would that save up energy for more important things?*

## When our minds multitask on their own

When we looked at multitasking in the previous section, we focused on outer factors that may cause us to get distracted. The fascinating thing with the human mind is that it can start multitasking by itself, without any outer disturbances. We can sit in a quiet room on our own, and suddenly our mind goes off thinking about something totally irrelevant to what we are doing. If you experience this often, don't worry – you are not alone.

In 2010, Harvard psychologists Matthew Killingsworth and Daniel Gilbert conducted a study[6] with over 2,000 respondents who got a special app installed on their smartphone. At random times of the day, a signal went off and respondents were supposed to answer a few questions. The first question was: "what are you doing right now?". Directly after that followed the questions: "what were you thinking of when the signal went off?".

Forty-seven percent of the time, respondents reported thinking about something else than they were doing. Similar studies have indicated the same thing; an untrained mind wanders, meaning that about half of the time, we are not fully focused on what we are doing.

In the mentioned study, participants were also asked to what extent they found themselves being present and focused on the meeting they were attending. Seventy percent answered that they on a regular basis found it difficult to be mentally present in the meeting they attended.

Imagine that you were responsible for a production facility that was only producing the things it was supposed to do half of the time it. You would probably want to do something to improve that ratio. Well, that is how our untrained mind typically works, so from a productivity point of view, there is a good business case for training and cultivating our ability to be present and focused.

Besides, being a challenge for our productivity, mind wandering can also affect our sense of well-being. Killingsworth's and Gilbert's research indicates that a wandering mind is often a worrying mind.[7] This is in line with the theme from the book *Why Zebras Don't Get Ulcers* by Robert Sampolsky I mentioned earlier. Humans do get ulcers, largely because we have the ability to ruminate about things that happened in the past and worry about things that may happen in the future.

When our minds wander, it tends to often be about things that we perceive as negative or threatening. This is another built-in survival mechanism in our brain, but it doesn't necessarily make us happy. Research therefore suggests a correlation between being more focused and feeling less worry and anxiety.

A final argument for practicing our ability to be focused is that it can help us get into the so-called flow state, or 'the zone' as it is often called in sports. I earlier mentioned Mihaly Csikszentmihalyi, a professor of psychology who studied happiness and creativity at the University of Chicago. Csikszentmihalyi found that people often perform well when they engage in things that give them the right challenge related to their skills.

If we don't get challenged enough, we can get bored. If the challenge is too great compared to our capabilities, we can get overwhelmed and anxious. But with the right balance, we can get into a flow state where we are totally absorbed in what we are doing, time disappears – and we are often very effective. Most of us have experienced this when practicing a sport, playing an instrument and hopefully even at work.

To achieve these flow states, we must engage with tasks that offer us the right level of challenge, and we need to be fully focused. Our ability to fully present with what we are doing increases the likelihood that we get into that productive and stress-free feeling of flow.

So, with all these benefits to being focused, is it possible to improve our focusing abilities? In our next section, we are going to explore some basic techniques used by people ranging from professional athletes to top executives.

## Attention training – improving our ability to be present and focused

Given what our work life looks like today, there has been an increasing interest in the research community around how we can train ourselves to be more present, focused and effective.

One answer to this question comes from what might be an unexpected source: the ancient practice of meditation. When I mention meditation, you may get associations to religious gurus and people sitting in lotus positions. It is true that meditation has been a practice in many spiritual traditions for centuries. But over the last decades, and thanks to contemporary science, meditation is also moving into mainstream as a secular mental training technique.

If we go back to some of the root meanings of the word for meditation in ancient languages such as Pali and Sanskrit, it refers to 'getting to know the mind' and 'cultivation of the mind'. In other words, long before modern psychology and the instruments we have today for doing research on the human brain, meditation techniques were used to understand the working of our minds and how to cultivate helpful states of mind.

On a personal note, I would say that no other habit has had such a significant positive impact on my own life, both professionally and privately, as establishing a daily meditation routine. This regular mental workout has provided both stress relief and mental clarity, but also enabled deeper self-awareness and better emotional regulation. A few minutes of dedicated practice of mindfulness each day has in my experience laid the foundation for many of the other capabilities we explore in this book.

There are thousands of different meditation techniques, but the one that probably has won the greatest impact in our modern society is what is called mindfulness meditation. The term mindfulness runs the risk of being overused these days, and just as with meditation, you may have positive or negative associations to word itself. But being mindful just means being present and attentive to what is going on.

Jon Kabat-Zinn,[8] one of the first to bring mindfulness into modern medicine back in the late 1970s, offers what he calls his working definition of mindfulness:

*Mindfulness is the awareness that arises through paying attention, on purpose, in the present moment, and without judgement*

The opposite of being mindful would be to be mindless, walking around on autopilot, not paying attention to what is happening around us and driven by our unconscious biases and judgments. Looking at it from that perspective, I guess most of us would rather be seen as mindful than mindless.

So, if mindfulness can be defined as a state of being focused, present and open-minded, what is mindfulness meditation? Well, that is just a specific training technique to improve our ability to get into a mindful state of mind. If you still struggle to relate to the word mindfulness, you can also think of mindfulness meditation as attention training. Going forward, I will use the terms interchangeably.

Later in this book, we will explore a broader range of benefits and ways to use mindfulness practice, but for starters we will look at two crucial faculties of the mind we cultivate when practicing mindfulness meditation:

- Focus – our ability to deliberately direct our attention to a chosen object.
- Awareness – our ability to be aware of what is going on around us as well as inside us.

Laser sharp focus without the ability to be aware of what is happening in our surrounding environment can lead to tunnel vision. We need a wider awareness to be able to discern what is most important for us to direct our attention to at any given moment.

However, being highly sensitive to the world around us, without the ability to focus on the task in front of us can make us easily distracted and ineffective.

The core idea of mindfulness/attention training is therefore to practice both these mental 'muscles' – focus and awareness – in parallel.

## The mechanics of mindfulness training

So how do we do this? We simply start by choosing an object to rest our attention on. It can be a picture, a sound or a physical sensation such as our breath. Breath is often used as the focus point and 'anchor' in mindfulness training for many reasons we will get back to later in this book. For starters, some of the good reasons for using your breath as your anchor of attention is that it is free, and it is always with you.

Once you have chosen the object for your attention, let us say your breath, the first part of your practice is to just rest your attention on the sensation of breathing.

After a few seconds, your mind will start wandering, and that is <u>not</u> a problem. Actually, that is what our minds naturally do. On average, we can focus our attention somewhere between 5 and 15 seconds before our thoughts wander off. This is to be expected and not a problem. It is the next move, that is, the key.

The moment you realise that your mind is wandering, congratulate yourself on detecting that, and kindly but firmly return your attention to your breath again. It will stay there for a few moments before it wanders off again, and then you bring it back again.

In this context, it can be helpful to use the analogy of going to the gym. Imagine that we are at the gym and want to strengthen our biceps muscles. If we grab a dumbbell and just hold it still for a few minutes we wouldn't get much of a workout. What we do when we train our physical muscles is to put stress on our muscle and then release it again. In the gym, we call this 'doing reps'.

In the mental gym of attention training, it works in similar ways. The moment we start mind-wandering, the attention 'muscle' loosens. We notice that and bring our attention back again – we just did one rep in the mental gym. A few seconds later, we lose our focus and bring it back again – we just did another rep.

What happens inside our brain is that the various neural networks related to our awareness and attention switch on and off as we do the practice. Every time we reestablish our focus, the neurons in these related networks fire together, and as the neuroscientists say, when neurons fire together, they wire together. Over time, these crucial networks will grow

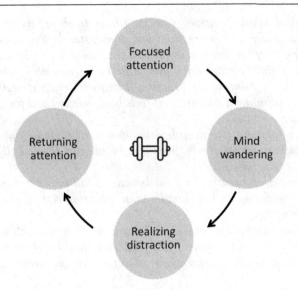

*Figure 1.2* The process of attention training.

stronger. So, if you find your mind wandering a lot when you try this exercise, don't worry – as long as you remember to bring your attention back again, you are just getting more exercise!

The last decades of neuroscience have shown that our brain is plastic, i.e. it will change according to how we use it. Just like our physical muscles shrink or grow according to how much we use them, the various networks of our brain can literally grow and become stronger by activating them.

Since the start of the 2000s, thousands of scientific studies have been conducted on the effects of mindfulness meditation, many of them using functional MR scanners that can measure brain activity. The findings clearly indicate that attention training grows the networks in our brain related to focus, self-awareness, and emotional regulation.[9]

If you don't already have a mindfulness practice that works for you, here are some basic pointers you can use for guidance:

- *Find a place where you can be sure to be undisturbed for the length of your practice. Once you get more experienced with mindfulness training, you can do it in busy places as well, but for a starter it is easier if you find a reasonably quiet place.*
- *Set a timer for the number of minutes you would like to practice. A tip here is to start small. Rather go for one minute to start with. If that works, you can increase to two minutes and build it from there.*

- *Find a comfortable position. You don't have to sit in any special pose. You can actually do this practice lying down, standing or even walking. The easiest way though is normally to start with sitting in a chair with both feet solidly on the floor and your back reasonably straight. To avoid dozing off during the practice, it helps to sit up straight without tensing. Try finding a posture that feels both relaxed and focused at the same time.*
- *Start with taking a few deep breaths and notice where you can sense your breathing most clearly. This can be in your lower belly, in your chest or at your nostrils.*
- *After a few deep breaths, let your breathing fall into a natural rhythm without interfering with it. Just let your attention rest on the sensation of breathing.*
- *When your mind wanders, remember not to beat yourself up or start analysing why that happened. Just smile, let go of the thought that distracted you and gently return your attention to your breath again, and again.*
- *If you find it very difficult to keep your attention on the subtle sensation of your breath, you can experiment with counting your outbreaths. Try counting to 10 and then down to 1 again. If you lose track of your counting, just start again....*

When your timer rings, take a moment to take stock of how you feel. Can you notice any difference in yourself, mentally or physically, compared to when you started the exercise?

The point here is not that you are supposed to reach any special state when you are doing your practice. We are all different, and as with physical exercise, our experiences will differ from time to time. However, chances are that when we take a few minutes to just focus our attention on the breath, we experienced some sense of relaxation and clarity of mind. If we compare our mind to a snow globe, we can get a feeling that our thoughts, just like snowflakes, settle to the ground as we stop shaking the globe. If you can recognise any of these experiences, it indicates that you have activated the parasympathetic nervous system we talked about earlier. Your body and mind have switched over to recovery mode for a moment.

Another common experience is feeling drowsy and even falling asleep. Again, don't worry, as this is a natural effect of your system starting to calm down. When we turn our attention inwards, our body tends to signal its needs. If you feel sleepy, your body is just telling you it would like some more sleep. Doing the practice at times when you are reasonably well rested makes it easier to explore the balance between being focused and relaxed.

If this basic mindfulness practice feels interesting and helpful for you, I invite you to experiment with creating a habit of doing a few minutes of attention training each day. It normally helps to find a regular time and place during the day that suits you and where you can be undisturbed. I often get the question of what the minimal viable doses is to get positive changes in our brain. There are studies indicating that a little over ten minutes a day of meditation can generate positive effects on attention, memory, emotional regulation and more.[10] Other studies suggest that meditation over time generates measurable changes to our brains.[11] Just like when we go to the physical gym, our muscles don't grow after a few rounds of practice. We must stick to our routine for a while before we can notice the differences.

That being said, even with just a few minutes a day, most people notice positive results on their well-being after only a couple of weeks of practice. So, start small, and build your habit from there. If you are new to this practice, it can be very helpful to use apps for guidance. There are plenty of free apps available, and many paid-for apps with professional content and guidance. In the reference section is a list of a few apps I can recommend.[12]

## Resetting to calm during busy days

Let's say that you have a problem with your computer, and you call the IT helpdesk. What is the first question they are going to ask you? Most likely something like: "Have you tried restarting?" For us human beings to function well, we too may need to 'restart' every now and then to function well. In this section, we will look at various techniques that can help us 'reset to calm', i.e. let our brain and nervous system settle a bit before we start our next activity.

In the previous section, we explored attention training as a way to improve our ability to be focused, and also discussed how this practice has the positive side effect of activating our parasympathetic nervous system, making us calmer.

Practicing mindfulness has a much wider scope than being calm and focused. In later parts of this book, we will expand our understanding of mindfulness and how it relates self-leadership, working with complex problems and building trusting relations with others. Before we move on to that, we will stay on the topic of sustainable high performance and explore a few more tips for how to reset to calm in your everyday life.

Even if mindfulness meditation has been shown to be very effective, it might not suit your temperament or lifestyle to set off dedicated time every day to do this kind of practice. We will therefore look at how we can integrate the principles of mindfulness into things we are doing anyway, and still get some of the same benefits we would from a formal practice.

There are a few different things we can do to activate our parasympathetic nervous system and thereby contribute to a sense of calm and clarity. You will probably recognise these based on your own experience.

### Focusing attention

We can work with our attention muscle, also in everyday activities. When we allow ourselves to be fully focused on an activity, it lessens the stress on our brain, and we can be relaxed although active. This can be any kind of activity like playing an instrument, knitting or even doing the dishes. The point is that we do the opposite of multitasking. Instead of thinking about something else than we are doing, we are just fully present with the activity we are engaged in.

This kind of integrated mindfulness can be applied to any daily activity you do, like brushing your teeth or reading to your kids. Or imagine that next time you take a coffee break. Instead of just pouring caffeinated liquid into your body while checking your messages, how about focusing solely on your coffee? Smelling the aroma, feeling the warmth, tasting the nuances in this very cup of coffee. Dedicating your attention, if only for two minutes, might give a different experience to your coffee break.

### Breathing deeply

We have known this since we were kids; slow deep breathing calms us down. What happens on a neurological level is that we stimulate the vagus nerve, which regulates our heart rhythm and many other things.

There are many different techniques for breath work, and if you have ever practiced yoga you have probably experienced the positive effects of working with breathing techniques, called pranayama in the yogic traditions. Although we won't go into a deeper exploration of breathing techniques in this book, there are two simple tips that can be helpful if our goal is to calm down our nervous system.

The first tip is to breathe deep down in our belly, allowing our belly to be soft so the air can flow down into your body. The second tip is to make our outbreath longer than our inbreath. You can try counting to two on the inbreath, and four on the outbreath.

This simple breathing technique can be applied at any moment you want to reset to calm, for example, waiting for the elevator, at the start of a meeting, etc. You can do it totally stealth – no one will notice while you are re-centering yourself.

### Moving slowly

We can all recognise the body language and movement of a stressed person. When our fight or flight system is activated, we often become more fidgety and move faster. The interesting thing is that we can trick our nervous system by deliberately slowing down our movements. This sends a signal to our nervous system that danger is over, and we begin to calm down.

This has, of course, been known and used for millennia. Traditional practices such as tai chi and yoga use this fact. It is just recently that modern science has been able to study the physiological reasons why this has such a calming effect. But we don't have to pick up any of the mentioned practices to use this trick. We can just start by deliberately moving more slowly in everyday situations.

Next time you go to the bathroom or between meetings, try slowing down your pace a little bit and just feel your feet as you walk. A tip here is not to slow down too much, or people will start wondering what you are doing... Just find a pace that makes you feel a bit more relaxed. It might take a few seconds more to get to where you are going, but chances are that you will get there as a slightly calmer and more settled version of yourself.

### Putting it into practice

With these three areas explained, I would now invite you to explore how you could build small mindfulness moments into your day. What are things you are doing anyway, which you could do with full presence, maybe a bit more slowly than normal, and/or while breathing deeply?

Here are some suggestions for micro practices as inspiration:

- Take a minute or two during your commute to work where you just focus on your own breathing.
- While walking to your office, really pay attention to your surroundings. Notice the fresh air, the sounds around you, etc.
- While waiting for your computer to start, use the opportunity to take a few deep breaths.
- Walking between meetings, see if you can do that a bit more slowly than usual, and breathe more deeply.
- While having your lunch, can you avoid checking messages and just focus on enjoying your food?
- Etc...

## Building micro-pauses into our routine

As we discussed earlier with the 50/10 principles, we can improve our resilience and endurance by giving both our mind and our body regular breaks during the day. In the previous sections, we have explored a few techniques that help calm down our nervous system. Depending on your type of work or personality profile, there may be other kinds of breaks that are helpful for you.

Going outside, getting fresh air, and doing short walks in nature has been shown to have many positive effects. Same thing with any other physical movement such as taking the stairs or doing some stretching by your desk. Allow yourself to be creative here. The point to remember is that we are not wired to perform well for hours on end without a break. Allowing breaks throughout our day is both supportive for our well-being, but it also helps us to be a more focused, creative and open-minded version of ourselves.

## The power of the pause to enhance team performance

Many years ago, I met a leader who worked for a software company in Silicon Valley – a very performance-oriented work environment. This leader had experienced what many of us may recognise: team members entering meetings at the last minute, stressed and working on their laptop trying to finish something they were engaged in in their previous meeting.

The head of this management team had noticed that it often took the first ten minutes or so of every meeting before the team members had really tuned in, and they could start discussing the important stuff. He therefore suggested to his team to conduct an experiment. Going forward, the team would start their meetings with two minutes in silence. During these minutes, the team members would turn away from their devices and ask themselves two questions:

- *What am I mentally bringing with me that has nothing to do with this meeting?*
- *How can I best contribute to the meeting I am in now?*

The team leader told his colleagues, that if anyone after these two minutes of individual reflection felt that they were unable to focus and contribute to the meeting, they were free to leave. It would be more effective for them to go and finish whatever other business needed to be taken care of, than to waste everyone's time by not being focused.

This was, of course, quite a controversial suggestion, but the team agreed to try it out. When they evaluated the experiment a couple of weeks later, they realised an interesting thing. After implementing this routine, they could finish their meetings earlier. The two minutes of tuning in at the start of the meeting helped team members become more focused and they could move through their agenda points more efficiently.

Over the years, I have shared this interesting anecdote with leaders from many organisations. It seems like this idea of pausing before going into action resonates with many other leaders' experiences and I have learned how the power of the pause is practiced in many other contexts.

One such context is a large construction company that has implemented a 'take two' rule on their construction sites. Before starting any activity, workers would always take two minutes to check their safety equipment and scan the area around them to make sure no one was within the working radius of their machine. This simple routine had significantly reduced the number of incidents on the site.

Another powerful example is from working with the head of an emergency unit at a large hospital. He shared that when he and his team went into surgery, their ability to be calm and focused could literally means the difference between life and death for their patient. He therefore experimented with a similar method of gathering his team and taking a short moment to gather themselves before opening the doors to the operation room and going into action.

Most of us do not hold the life of others in our hands on a daily basis, but as leaders our actions can still have a lot of consequences for other people – short-term or long-term. Early in this book, we looked at how our cognitive functioning differs, depending on what neural mode we are in. To make good decisions that benefit both us and the greater whole, we might want to pause and 'reset to calm' every now and then. Just like professional athletes have routines to get themselves tuned in and focused before an important performance, we too can benefit from finding a 'pre-game' routine that works for us.

Resetting to calm for a moment can make it more likely that we show up as the leaders and people we would like to be. What do you think the effect would be if you and your colleagues leveraged the power of the pause, and took a short moment to settle and focus before you started your meetings or made important decisions?

## Self-compassion as support for resilience and growth

In this chapter, we have mainly focused on physiological and neurological aspects of sustainable high performance. But, it is relevant to revisit another perspective here as well – our own attitude toward ourselves and our own performance.

Just as taking breaks can seem counter-intuitive to be more productive and effective, self-compassion can also seem like an unexpected part of enhancing our performance. Many of us may consciously or subconsciously subscribe to the assumption that to develop ourselves and perform at our best, we need to be constantly self-critical. Interestingly, science shows differently.

Two of the world's leading researchers in this field are Kristin Neff and Chris Germer, both working out of the University of Texas. They have been studying how self-compassion correlates with our ability to learn and adapt, and I can recommend diving deeper into their work.[13] One of their main conclusions is that people who are self-compassionate are usually more resilient and adaptive.

The key here seems to be that when we are self-compassionate, i.e. not beating ourselves up for falling short, we are more willing to face reality and accept our shortcomings. In contrast, if we have a tendency to be very hard on ourselves, which puts us in painful emotional state, we will subconsciously avoid acknowledging when we do something wrong, in order to avoid that pain.

Self-compassion in this context is not about being soft on ourselves, but to see things clearly and at the same time apply a supportive approach. It is extending the same attitude to ourselves, as we would have toward a good friend who needs support.

Kristine Neff often defines self-compassion in three steps:

### Mindfulness

Becoming aware of our patterns and the stories we tell ourselves (this correlates with Modupe Akinola's point about how our mental framing influences our stress).

### Common humanity

Connecting to the fact that failing is part of being human. When we are too caught up in our own self-criticism, we can miss the fact that everyone else around us also makes mistakes and have their shortcomings.

### Applying kindness

Approaching ourselves in a way that is supportive. This does not mean feeling sorry for ourselves, but asking what we could do to improve the situation for ourselves and others.

As you explore how you can build micro-breaks into your workday to build your endurance and resilience, you can also try giving your inner critic a break during the day. By applying Neff's three principles, you can soften the unnecessary pressure you might be putting on yourself.

The next time you feel self-criticism rising in you, pause and reflect on these questions:

- *What is the story I am telling myself right now?*
- *Is my self-talk useful and helpful?*
- *If I take a bigger perspective on this situation, how serious is my short-coming?*
- *Would other people judge me as hard as I do?*
- *What would I tell a good friend who was in the same situation as I am?*
- *What is the best thing I can do right now, to improve the situation?*

The term psychological safety is used to describe the atmosphere in teams where people feel safe to be themselves, can be honest without repercussions and feel supported if they make a mistake. This atmosphere has been shown to be a key element in high-performing and innovative teams (more about this in later sections). Self-compassion can be understood as the internal version of psychological safety. Once we can relax with ourselves, we are often more able to see things clearly and take skillful action.

### Creating a culture that supports sustainable high performance

Our work cultures can at times manifest the opposite of some of the ideas and principles we have explored in this first chapter. If that is the case for you, you might want to reflect on whether the traditions and habits you currently have are helpful, or if they could use an upgrade. If you are in a leadership position, you probably have more influence than you think on what your work culture could look like going forward.

If what we covered so far in this book makes sense to you, I hope you feel inspired to experiment with some of the ideas. Most of what we discussed you can experiment with on your own, but you may also want to explore integrating some of the principles in your team and organisation. Here are some questions to reflect on:

- *Given what neuroscience tells us about how our brain works, how could we arrange our work smarter?*
- *Would it be helpful to share this kind of knowledge with others to help people perform better and be sustainable over time?*

- *How could we use our technology more wisely?*
- *How could we run our meetings in a way that helps everyone to be more present, focused and open-minded?*
- *How could we create a culture where it would be normal and encouraged to take short breaks and 'reset to calm' every now and then?*

People and organisations are different, so you will have to find out what works for you and your team. Good luck with your exploration. I hope it will help you toward creating a sustainable work environment where people will be able to show up fully and thrive.

## Notes

1 A.J. Crum, J.P. Jamieson and M. Akinola (2020). Optimizing stress: An integrated intervention for regulating stress responses. *Emotion*, 20(1), 120–125. doi: 10.1037/emo0000670. Akinola is also featured in series on how to 'stress better' in the podcast and app *Ten Percent Happier*. To learn more about her work, check out modupeakinola.com.
2 Carol Dweck, *Mindset: The New Psychology of Success* (2006).
3 Robert Sapolsky, *Why Zebras Don't Get Ulcers* (1994).
4 Potential Project works with integrating contemplative practices and mind training in organisations. Rasmus Hougaard and Jaqueline Carter have together with their colleagues published several practical books on the topic: *One Second Ahead* (2016), *The Mind of the Leader* (2018), *Compassionate Leadership* (2022). Find out more about their research on potentialproject.com.
5 Mihaly Csikszentmihalyi, *Flow: The Psychology of Optimal Experience* (1990).
6 Matthew A. Killingsworth and Daniel T. Gilbert (2010). A wandering mind is an unhappy mind. *Science* 12, 330(6006), 932.
7 You can find an article on the research done by Matthew Killingsworth and Daniel Gilbert, by searching for: news.harvard.edu/gazette/story/2010/11/wandering-mind-not-a-happy-mind.
8 Jon Kabat-Zinn is a professor emeritus of medicine, and the creator of the maybe most well-known secular meditation program in the world called Mindfulness Based Stress Reduction (MBSR). He has authored many books on mindfulness, the most popular *Full Catastrophe Living* (1990) and *Wherever You Go, There You Are* (1994). Kabat-Zinn's books can be recommended for anyone who would like an introduction to mindfulness and meditation. You can find more information on jonkabat-zinn.com.
9 Yi-Yuan Tang, Hölzel, Posner, *The Neuroscience of Mindfulness Meditation* (2015). nature.com/nrn/journal/v16/n4/abs/nrn3916.
10 J.C. Basso, A. McHale, V. Ende, D.J. Oberlin and W.A. Suzuki (2019). Brief, daily meditation enhances attention, memory, mood, and emotional regulation in non-experienced meditators. *Behavioural Brain Research*, 356, 208–220. doi: 10.1016/j.bbr.2018.08.023. pubmed.ncbi.nlm.nih.gov/30153464/.
11 S.W. Lazar et al., *Meditation Experience Is Associated with Increased Cortical Thickness* (2005). B.K. Holzel et al., *Stress Reduction Correlates with Structural Changes in the Amygdala* (2010). ncbi.nlm.nih.gov/pmc/articles/PMC2840837.

12  Among the most popular paid-for apps with plenty of inspiration, teachings and guided practices are: *Ten Percent Happier*, *Waking Up*, *Calm* and *Headspace*. They often offer partly free content or a free trial period. You can also search for free apps with basic functions such as meditation timers and short guided practices on the app store of your device.
13  Kristin Neff and Chris Germer have gathered a lot of resources on this homepage: self-compassion.org. You fill find references to research as well as guided practices and more.

# Chapter 2

# Staying smart under pressure

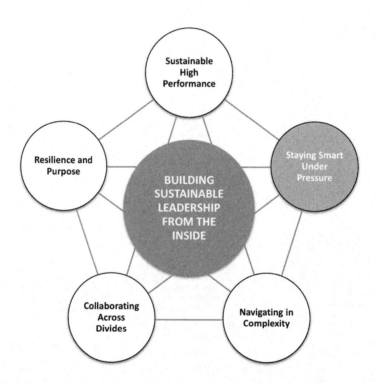

*Figure 2.1* The five areas of building sustainable leadership from the inside.

## Overview Chapter 2: Staying smart under pressure

Building on part 1, we go further into understanding neurological and psychological dynamics that influence how we show up in daily

DOI: 10.4324/9781003485148-3

life. We unpack how emotions work and how we can develop our ability to navigate them skilfully.

Besides improving our impulse control, we also explore how developing self-awareness and having the ability to pause and reflect plays an important role in succeeding with any type of change. We introduce several frameworks and practical exercises for increasing self-awareness and enabling self-leadership.

*These are some of the areas we are going to cover:*

- Principles for maintaining a balanced mind
- Exploring different levels of self-awareness
- Learning about our early warning signs
- Self-compassion as a catalyst for deeper self-awareness
- Self-leadership and impulse control
- Pausing our autopilot to make space for wise choices
- Working with awareness-based change
- The gradual development of self-leadership

*Example of how this part links to and supports other sections:*

- In this chapter, we introduce basic practices for increasing self-awareness, which we will build on in the later chapters. Self-awareness runs as a theme through all parts of the book, and is a key element in Navigating in Complexity, Collaborating across Divides as well as Resilience.
- Self-leadership and impulse control covered in this chapter help us build the so-called 'negative capability', crucial for *Navigating in Complexity*. It is also key to regulating emotions which can come in handy when *Collaborating across Divides*.
- The sections in this chapter on self-compassion and awareness-based change are also related to the part of the book where we explore Resilience and Purpose.

*Supporting audio material:*
There are guided audio practices accompanying this chapter. Search for *Meditations for Leaders (Joakim Eriksson)* to find them on your preferred audio platform.

## Self-leadership – navigating in the gap between knowing and doing

Most of us have a self-image of how we would like to show up and act in the different roles we take on in our life, as a leader, parent, spouse, etc. And then in the midst of daily life, especially when we feel stressed, we sometimes find ourselves getting hi-jacked by our emotions or repeating old behavioral patterns that we know are not helpful. We experience a gap between what we know as the right thing to do, and what we end up doing. If you can recognise yourself in this, congratulations – you are perfectly normal.

Our brain is hard wired to save mental energy by having much of our thinking and behaviors run on autopilot and to trigger emotional reactions to activate self-protection. But even if these mental functions have been beneficial from an evolutionary perspective, they can also be problematic in modern life when we must adapt to new circumstances or handle complex situations.

To live and act in line with who we would like to be and what we know to be right requires developing our emotional intelligence, so we can understand and acknowledge our impulses and emotions, but not be ruled by them. Cultivating these skills increases our ability to stay composed and act with some level of consciousness also when things are difficult. If we are in some kind of position of leadership or authority, these skills become crucial. As role models, the way we act will influence others and set the benchmark for the culture in the organisation.

Later in this chapter, we will explore different ways to develop emotional intelligence and impulse control, to help us stay smart under pressure and show up as the version of ourselves we would like to be.

## Succeeding with conscious change

Besides making us better at handling stressful situations, there is also a larger perspective to why self-awareness and self-leadership are important leadership capabilities.

When I got my first C-level position and became a part of a management team, I noticed something interesting. We could process a business issue in our team, look at the facts and discuss alternative solutions. After a while, we would come to a decision and everyone around the table would agree on the necessary actions. And then, a couple of weeks later when we met again, things had rarely moved forward a lot.

Although we had made a rational decision and together agreed on the next action steps, there seemed to be an invisible hand holding us back from actually acting on it. Now, the question is if the lack of action was due to lack of clarity? If we produced more PowerPoint-slides or spread sheets to back up our action plan, would that make things happen? Sometimes more clarity did the trick, but often not.

Metaphorically, it seemed that things tended to get stuck somewhere on the way from the head to the heart and to the hands. Intellectually we knew what to do, but subconscious competing commitments and habitual patterns kept us from acting on it with the focus it required.

Slowly it dawned on me that the key to change and development, both personal and organisational, seems to lie in that gap between knowing and doing. All our analysis and action plans aren't of much use if we cannot pair it with self-awareness and self-leadership.

Earlier in the book, we referred to behavioral psychologist Daniel Kahneman and what he calls System 1 and System 2. When System 1 rules (which it does most of the time) our thoughts and actions are likely to be guided by subconscious and habitual mental patterns, resulting in us repeating previous behaviors. To make more conscious choices and implement new behaviors, we must engage System 2.

Succeeding with any change and transformation, whether on a personal, organisational or even societal level, requires us to learn to recognise the habitual thinking and behavioral patterns associated with what Kahneman calls System 1, and to deliberately engage System 2 – our conscious, rational, and reflected self. In the following chapter, we will look at how we can train ourselves to engage System 2 and switch from autopilot to more conscious action. The potential applications for this are many:

- We can start closing the gap between who we aspire to be as leaders, and how we show up in daily life.
- When under pressure, we can avoid being hi-jacked by emotions and fall into unskillful behavioral patterns.
- In periods of change and transformation, we can increase our ability to integrate the necessary new behaviors and ways of working.

To deliberately engage System 2 and act with consciousness requires us to cultivate mental balance. Let us explore what that means.

## Principles for maintaining a balanced mind

As human beings, we must accept that we regularly will get triggered and brought out of balance by events around us. To think we will always be cool and composed is quite utopian. However, we can train ourselves to regain balance more quickly, every time we lose it. We can compare this to how we ride a bicycle.

I guess most of you reading this know how to ride a bike. What you may not think about is that when you are riding your bike, you are always about to lose your balance. At any given moment, your balance is a little bit off to the left or the right. This is normally not a problem, since when you are riding, you will constantly be making micro-corrections that keep you up straight.

If you have kids around you who are learning to ride their bike, you will notice it is a bit more wobbly. They are swaying back and forth, and sometimes go off the road. But then one day they get it. They somehow stop swaying and go straight – a proud moment for any parent.

What is it we learn as kids when we learn to ride a bicycle, and what is the relevant parallel to maintaining a balanced mind? There are two key elements to learn to ride a bike:

- We have to sense what it feels like when we start to lose balance so we can respond quickly.
- We must learn what is the appropriate counter measure to compensate and keep the up straight.

To maintain a balanced mind, we must:

- Learn to recognise the signals indicating that we are starting to 'lose balance', i.e. get too emotional or acting in a manner that is not helpful.
- Learn techniques for how to defuse our reaction, and bring ourselves 'back to balance' again.

A key point in comparing mental balance with riding a bicycle is that the earlier we can notice that we are off balance, the less we will have to adjust. Therefore, in the coming sections, we are going to explore different ways to cultivate our capacity for situational self-awareness. Following that, we will look at practices for how to apply impulse control and emotional regulation.

## Self-awareness – drawing a map of ourselves

If you ever tried orienteering or navigating at sea, you know it helps having a good map or sea chart. The more detailed map you have, the easier it is to find an efficient way forward. You can see where there are challenges to avoid, and where you can travel more easily.

Building our self-awareness over time works the same way. The more we learn about ourselves, the better we will know what situations trigger us, when we are at our best and where to be careful. To stay with the metaphor of the map for a moment, when we get lost it is easier to figure out where we are when we have clear reference points marked out on our map. The same way we when we 'get lost' in an emotional reaction, we can more easily recognise that and know how to handle it if we have worked diligently on developing our self-awareness.

### Personality profiles – learning about our general traits and preferences

If you have been in the job market for a while, you have likely already filled out one or more personality assessment questionnaires, such as MBTI, DISC, Insight, Lumina, Hogan, etc. There are many tools on the market that can help us understand the key elements of our basic personality traits. In this book, we will not go deeper into exploring different personality assessments, but for the sake of 'drawing a map' of ourselves, I just want to point out that used skilfully, these assessments can be a rich source of information for your 'map'.

If you have one or more profile reports saved somewhere, it can be worthwhile to dig them out and explore the data. Are there any clear patterns across assessments? What can you recognise in your everyday life? Are the assessments indicating different patterns or behaviors depending on the scenario, for example, when you are in control or when you are stressed?

When receiving a personality profile report, it is important to remember that it is an indication of your personality, not the truth about you. It is wise to take the feedback the report provides seriously as it can often be surprisingly precise, but also remember that all assessment tools are based on theoretical models and don't necessarily give the full picture of you as a human being.

Approached with openness and curiosity, personality assessments can help you with sketching the overall elements of your self-awareness map. The next step is to start exploring the nuances and how the different aspects of our personality show up in different contexts.

### Exploring situational self-awareness

No matter if we are dominantly introverted or extroverted, focused on details or big picture thinkers, we don't show up as the same person all the time. Our current emotional and mental state will vary from day to day and moment to moment, influencing how we think, speak and act.

Neuroscientist Robert Sapolsky has a fascinating way of describing how a long chain of circumstances and events influences how we act in any given moment.[1] He makes the case that who we are and how we act is the result of things ranging from the culture we have grown up in, the education we have and the peers we socialise with, but also what has happened to us over the last couple of days, how we have slept the night before, what we have eaten the same day and what hormones are dominating our system at this very moment. All these interacting elements determine how we will respond to a given situation.

Working with self-awareness both entails knowing the larger outlines of our personality, but also paying attention to our mental state moment to moment. Like when riding a bike, we must keep paying attention to our balance. The good news here is that situational awareness is a trainable skill. We can practice our ability to notice even subtle changes in our mind and mood, and thereby be able to navigate in it more skilfully.

### Self-compassion as support for growing our self-awareness

To be able to look really honestly at ourselves with all our potential and strengths as well as our human flaws, we have to bring a good dose of self-compassion into the picture. As you may remember from the previous chapter, research by Kristin Neff and Chris Germer has shown that applying a kind attitude toward ourselves doesn't make us deny our shortcomings but supports more honest self-assessment.

A useful expression in this context is *fierce self-compassion*. It may sound like an oxymoron, but it points to the paradoxical combination of brutal honesty and kindness and compassion that we need to build true resilience.

If we shy away from looking at the less flattering sides of ourselves, they may pop up when we least expect them and ruin the party. If we, on the other hand tend to beat ourselves up for not being perfect, we will probably avoid looking at our weaknesses or stay away from challenging situations where we risk failing.

True resilience comes from being deeply grounded in who we are. When we have had the courage to look around in the different corners of our personality and know what is there, we will experience fewer surprises. We don't have to spend so much energy on protecting or hiding our weaknesses but can direct that energy toward growth and development.

To get comfortable with both 'the good, the bad and the ugly' parts of our own personalities, we need to be able to look at them with soft eyes. As Neff puts it, we can see our shared humanity in both our strengths and shortcomings and have the motivation to grow from there. With this fierce self-compassion in mind, we will in the coming sections explore a few practices that can help you notice more details about your own personality, preferences and patterns.

## Learning to recognise our early warning signs

In a popular TED talk on cultivating collaboration, the former judge Jim Tamm[2] talks about learning your 'early warning signs' as it can help you catch yourself early and avoid derailing into less helpful behavior.

Going back to our metaphor of riding a bike, the better we are at reading our early warnings signs, the quicker we can catch ourselves when we start to lose our mental balance. There are different ways to increase awareness about our own early warning signs and we will explore three different methods.

### Physical sensations as the first indicator

We have earlier talked about the two mental operating modes that Daniel Kahneman calls System 1 and System 2. Using neuroscientific language, these modes can roughly be correlated to two different regions of the brain called the limbic system (System 1) and the prefrontal cortex (System 2).

The limbic system is sometimes called the emotional brain. Most of the activity in our limbic system is subconscious, but this part of our brain stores important information and experiences relating to what is good for us, what should be interpreted as a threat, and how we should act to stay safe. Based on this, our limbic system constantly scans incoming data from our environment and signals us when we should respond to something. The way the limbic system communicates its messages to us is through emotions. Emotions in this context can be understood as physiological sensations in our body, triggered by signals from our limbic system. It can be a sucking feeling in our belly, tension in our jaw, or our hands sweating.

In 2013, a team of Finnish neuroscientists lead by Lauri Nummenmaa conducted a study indicating that emotions can be correlated with certain physiological sensation.[3] Seven hundred respondents from both Western Europe and East Asia were shown words, stories, movies, facial expressions, etc., to trigger emotional reactions. The subjects were asked to notice where they could sense changes in activity in their own body while watching the different stimuli.

Subjects were then given blank silhouettes of a human body and asked to colour where in their bodies they experienced increased or decreasing activity. When the researchers accumulated the data, they could see clear patterns across cultures for where in the body the subjects had experienced, for example, joy, anger, disgust, anxiety, etc. The key take-away from this study was that there seems to be clear physiological sensations and experiences related to specific emotions.

Other research experiments have indicated that when emotions are triggered in us, the physiological sensations associated with this emotion show up in our body before we cognitively begin to realise that we are having an emotional reaction. This can be a very useful insight if we are to develop an early warning system.

Imagine you are getting irritated in a meeting. Before you realise this cognitively, chances are that your cheeks have already started blushing, your forehead is frowning, and the tone of your voice has changed. You may miss these signals if you are deeply engaged in the conversation. But your colleagues may actually notice you reacting before you realise it yourself.

Starting to pay attention to bodily sensations in our everyday life can be an excellent way to tune up your early warning system. Your body often mirrors what is going on in your mind, even if it is subconscious. This can give you a heads-up before you start acting out an emotional reaction unwillingly.

For some, physiological sensations related to emotions can be very clear, especially with certain emotional states. For others, there may only be very subtle physiological reactions. Our ability to notice these subtle changes in ourselves is, however, a segway into increased self-awareness and it is a trainable skill.

### Practicing noticing physical sensations

A key part of our brain related to our capacity for noticing our emotional states is called the insula. The insula can be activated and trained by specific practices, which then gives us an enhanced ability to read our own mental and emotional state at any moment. One such 'insula workout' is to systematically go through our body and notice different sensations.

If you have ever practiced yoga, it is likely that you have tried some version of a body scan. A positive side effect of a body scan is usually a sense of relaxation. Just like we explored in the earlier section on micro-recovery, resting our attention on our breath and/or our body normally helps us activate the parasympathetic nervous system and makes us feel more relaxed.

The main focus for the body scan exercise below is however not on relaxation, but on strengthening awareness of what sensations are present in different parts of our body. When we in the previous chapter introduced you to the principles of attention training or mindfulness meditation, we used our breath as the focus point for our attention. In the body scan, we instead deliberately move our attention from one part of the body to the next, noticing what is there without trying to change anything.

Here is a simple guide to doing a body scan:

- *Find a comfortable position, this can be sitting, lying down or even standing up. The advantages to sitting rather than lying down in this context is that it reduces the risk of dozing off...*
- *Start by taking a few deep breaths where you notice the air passing in and out and allow your body to relax as it wants on the out-breaths.*
- *Start with feeling your feet. Notice what sensations there are. Maybe you can feel the contact with the floor, with your shoes or any other sensation.*
- *Let your attention slowly move up into your ankles and lower legs. Same question – what can you notice?*
- *Move on to your knees and upper legs. Any aches, tensions, or other sensations?*
- *Explore the area of your butt and hip. If you are sitting, what does the contact with the chair feel like? What other sensations can you notice in this area of the body?*
- *Let your attention move up into the lower belly and lower back. Can you feel the movement of your breath here? What else can you notice?*
- *Explore the solar plexus area and the middle of your back.*
- *Now pay attention to your chest and upper back. Any tension here or other sensations?*

- *Become aware of your shoulders. A place where we often store tension. How are your shoulders doing right now? You do not have to change anything, just notice what is there.*
- *Let your attention go out into your upper arms, through the elbows and into your lower arms.*
- *Notice your hands. Can you feel your hands without looking at them or moving them? What sensations can you notice in your hands?*
- *Now, let your awareness be with your throat and neck. How relaxed or tense is it?*
- *Feel the back, sides and top of your head.*
- *Now, feel your face. We have over 40 muscles in our face. How are they right now? What part of your face is tensed, and what part is relaxed.*
- *Finally, allow your awareness to take in all your body from your feet to the top of your head. What can you notice in your body right now?*

Scanning our body step by step like this, both practices our attention muscle, but also makes us more aware about what signals might be there to pay attention to. When you have done this practice a few times, you will likely notice that you more easily pick up on subtle sensations and changes in your physical state, also when you are not doing formal practice. You have primed your insula to be more sensitive.

To learn more about your emotional patterns and add data to your self-awareness map, there is also an additional element you can add to the body scan practice. After you have tuned into your body, you can try thinking about different scenarios in your life that usually evokes some kind of emotion. It can be moments that usually make you feel happy or inspired, or situations where you often get irritated or anxious.

By just bringing these situations to mind, we can often sense our body reacting to the memory. Sitting in a calm and safe space, we can explore what the emotions related to these situations feel like in our body. It can be very subtle sensations of tension in our face, or a strong experience of heart rate going up and muscles tensing. Although this is not necessarily a pleasant experience, simulating scenarios in our mind and noticing the related bodily sensations can give us useful clues to what our physical early warning signs are. This, in turn, can be helpful knowledge if we want to pause an emotional reaction before it goes too far.

### Journaling and flow-writing as tool for increasing self-awareness

Another helpful tool to increase our self-awareness is to practice journaling, i.e. writing down our thoughts and reflections. If you are like me, this may not be your preferred way of processing your thoughts, but I have learned that there are some special benefits to this that are worth exploring. There is even research showing that journaling on a regular basis increases life satisfaction, general well-being, as well as clarity about priorities.[4]

Flow-writing is a dynamic version of journaling, which can spark the writing process for those of us who don't naturally go there. You set a timer for a couple of minutes and then use a prompt, for example, "what is on your mind right now?", to get your writing going. There are two principles to flow-writing; you start writing immediately when the timer starts, without pre-thinking what you are going to write, and you keep your pen moving until the timer rings.

This can feel a bit weird at the start as we are so used to 'think things through' before we write anything down. The aim with flow-writing, however, is to by-pass our inner editor and just let whatever thoughts, images and emotions that are in us flow out on paper. We do not worry about our handwriting, spelling or if what comes down on paper is 'smart' or not. We just brain-dump out on paper.

We can use any kind of question or sentence as a prompt to kick us off in a direction. But it is not important that what we write down ends up being directly related to the initial prompt. The role of the prompts is just to get us going. You can use one prompt and just keep writing for a few minutes based on that one, or you can work with string of different prompts and write, for example, two minutes on each.

When you finish your flow-writing, you take a moment to go through what has come down on paper. Read it with an open and curious attitude and take your time to underline words or sentences that you sense are especially interesting, surprising or relevant.

### Examples for flow-writing prompts

 Below are examples of general prompts that you can use. I would suggest you set a timer for around two minutes per prompt and allow your pen to flow, writing down whatever shows up in your mind. Research indicates that writing with a pen works better than a keyboard, but you are welcome to explore what works for you.

- *What is on my mind right now is…*
- *What I am inspired by is…*
- *What I am struggling with is…*
- *Things that bring me out of balance are…*
- *What feels important to me is…*
- *I am at my best when I…*

To notice and analyse our own thought processes can be difficult, when we are trying to do it all in our mind. This is why journaling and flow-writing can be an interesting complementary tool for self-exploration. By letting our thoughts flow unedited out on paper, we can look at them more objectively. If you try journaling a couple of times, it is likely that you will start seeing some patterns in what comes down on paper. Journaling is a practical technique for increasing self-awareness and can help you add additional data to your map.

Apart from being a tool for self-awareness, flow-writing or journaling techniques can also be helpful in situations where you feel overwhelmed, confused or are facing a difficult decision. Taking a few minutes to write down the thoughts that swirl in your head, the pro's and con's of different solutions, etc., can sometimes create an overview and clarity that is helpful. We will revisit this technique later in the book when we explore the topic of navigating in complexity.

### Cultivating a learning mindset

In the last sections, we have looked at various ways of increasing our self-awareness over time, from using professional personality assessments to situational self-awareness, noticing emotions and physical sensations in our body.

No matter how well educated and smart we are, our personality and our moment-to-moment emotional state will influence how skilfully we apply our knowledge in real-life situations. By getting to know our own biases, patterns, and habits we can increasingly leverage what we know in ways that are helpful.

By cultivating an approach of curiosity, honesty and self-compassion, we can use our daily experiences as an ongoing process of learning and collecting data. This attitude also becomes the essence of having a learning and growth mindset, which we will return to in later chapters.

## Self-leadership and the art of responding consciously

Let us return for a moment to the comparison between mental balance and riding a bicycle. To maintain a balanced mind, we need to first of all notice when we are losing balance (self-awareness) and then be able to take the appropriate measures to regain our balance (self-regulation).

In the previous sections, we have explored different ways of increasing our self-awareness, i.e. knowing our typical derailers and what the early warnings are when we are starting to lose our mental balance. We will now shift our focus to the other part of the bicycle metaphor – how to bring back balance by regulating and adapting to the situation.

### At the heart of good leadership is the ability to be mindful and adaptive

Having worked over 15 years as a leadership consultant, I have read many meters of leadership literature and worked with thousands of leaders. If I would have to summarise the essence of good leadership in a simple sentence, it would probably be something like this:

*Leadership is the ability to sense what each situation calls for and apply just that.*

In this simple sentence lie two key abilities:

1  To be so present, mindful, and open that we can sense what the situation at hand really requires, which means seeing beyond our own biases, assumptions, and interpretations.
2  To be able to turn off our own autopilot behavior and adapt our actions to what is needed, even if that means breaking with our own personal preferences and habits.

This definition opens for a broader understanding of leadership than something that is limited to having a formal managerial position. No matter what roles we have in an organisation, a family or in society, we can all potentially take on leadership by seeing clearly what a situation calls for and step in and do whatever is in our range of influence and ability.

In the coming sections, we will explore ways to rise above our emotional autopilots and habitual behaviors to better be able to add 'what each situation calls for'.

### Forced action, in-action and conscious action

To apply the appropriate action in a given situation, we need to become aware of where our bias-based thinking and intuitive impulses tend to take us. We can use our impulses as valuable inputs, but we don't have to be ruled by them.

In a way, we can say that there potentially are three kinds of action in any situation:

- Forced action, where we react and behave based on habitual patterns or social norms
- In-action, where we get paralysed or when fear of failing keeps us from doing what is called for
- Conscious action, where we are able to read a situation clearly and respond in a productive way

Even if our automated thinking and behaviors save time and energy, conscious action is the key to breaking habits and succeeding with any kind of change and transformation, be it on an individual or organisational level.

### Creating some distance between ourselves and our impulses

As human beings, our thinking processes and emotional reactions are to a large degree automated, but our behaviors don't have to be. When we learn to notice our impulses without being ruled by them, we increase our flexibility of action and open for a greater repertoire of possibilities. Cultivating this flexibility starts with observing and learning how our mind works.

You have probably noticed that when you close your eyes for a few minutes, for example, when doing a mindfulness practice, your mind will produce a wide spectrum of impulses, thoughts, images, emotions, etc., with no apparent pattern between them. Trying to stop this natural output of the mind is like trying to change the weather.

We might not like the weather, but it will still be what it is. However, we can learn to observe our internal 'weather patterns' and be more conscious of how we act on them. When we get more experienced in our self-awareness practices, we can acknowledge our various thoughts, feelings, and impulses without being ruled by them. We can have emotions, without them having us.

In the English language, we identify with our emotions in a way. We say, for example, 'I am angry'. In other languages like Spanish, you would say 'I have anger'. A segway into greater emotional regulation and impulse control is to start relating to emotions, thoughts and impulses as something we have, not what we are. We can practice naming and labeling our recurring emotions and impulses instead of identifying with them.

Relating back to our section about self-awareness, the more we get familiar with our typical thoughts and emotions, the more easily we can avoid being hi-jacked by them and rather notice "oh, I am experiencing this emotion right now...". By creating a little distance between us and our emotions and impulses, we have created a space where we can make smarter choices.

### Situational awareness for increased adaptability

Does this mean that we always need to be calm and cool, no matter what happens around us? Is there no place for strong emotions? Many years ago, when I did the teacher training for the Search Inside Yourself program,[5] one of the founders of the program and an early Google engineer, Chade Meng-Tan, visited our training.

Meng always showed up calm and smiling and had this (almost irritating) aura of being calm and composed. We therefore asked him if he never got angry. He then shared a story about a time he was traveling and got to an airport to pick up his rental car. When signing the contract, he suddenly realised that the car rental company had tried to add extra charges for an insurance he explicitly had declined.

Meng described how he could notice anger rising in his body, but thanks to many years of practice, he could pause and ask himself "is this the right time to be angry". In that moment he decided, "yes it is!" So, he expressed his opinion in a colourful manner to the car rental representative....

The essence here is, of course, that impulse control is not about never giving voice to opinions and emotions but being able to do it for the right reasons, at the right time and in the right manner.

If we learn to build in 'a moment of choice' when we get triggered by something, we can use that moment to discern what the wise action in that moment is.

Austrian psychiatrist Victor Frankl was imprisoned in the concentration camps during World War II, and based on his experience, wrote the book *Man's Search for Meaning*.[6] His teachings were later summarised by Steven Covey in these sentences:

> *Between stimuli and response there is a space*
> *In that space lies our ability to choose our response*
> *In that lies the key to our happiness and freedom*

Our key to self-leadership and situational adaptability lies in creating and growing a little space and moment of choice. Even if it is only a second, it can be all it takes for a more conscious action. In the following sections, we will explore what happens in our brain when our emotions get the better of us, and how we can cultivate our ability to create that space for choice Frankl referred to.

### When we get hi-jacked by our amygdala

You may have heard about the expression 'amygdala hi-jack' for when our emotions overrule our rational thinking. The amygdala is a little almond-shaped part of our brain located in our limbic system. The amygdala has among other things the role of an alarm bell, continuously scanning for dangers and activating our fear-response when it detects something potentially threatening.

Thanks to our amygdala, Homo Sapiens is still around on this planet. From an evolutionary perspective, the amygdala has played a key role in helping us avoid dangers and survive as a species. Today most of us are facing more of what can be understood as social threats than physical dangers. We worry less about being eaten by predators, but more about succeeding with our career, being respected by our peers or getting enough likes on social media. But even if our challenges are different, our ancient amygdala still reacts to everything it perceives as a potential threat to our well-being.

At times we may think it is a bit tiring that this inner alarm bell gets us stressed up about things that turn out to be unimportant. But it is worth remembering that having a well-developed amygdala response has been rewarded by evolution. As one of the neuroscientists I studied with explained it; "our ancestors where the nervous monkeys, because the chill monkeys got eaten". Through many hundred thousand years of evolution, we had to be relatively paranoid and anxious to survive and have our genes passed on. So here we are, thousands of generations later, with a well-developed amygdala getting triggered by both important and trivial things.

Thankfully, evolution has also developed a regulatory system that helps balance the most paranoid reactions from the amygdala. Our prefrontal cortex, the executive center of our brain located just behind our forehead, analyses the warning signals from the amygdala and regulates our emotional reaction.

Let us take a scenario as an example. You get to work in the morning, and your boss doesn't say hello to you when you meet in the hallway. Your amygdala will likely interpret that as a potential problem (*I must have done something wrong…*) and sound the alarm bell. But your analytical pre-frontal cortex will probably put a perspective on the situation, recalling that your manager is preparing for a difficult meeting that day and was probably just in her own thoughts.

Throughout the day, there is an on-going dance between bottom-up warning signals coming from the amygdala and the top-down regulation from the more rational and analytical parts of our brain. But what happens when we get tired?

Let's say it is late afternoon. We haven't slept well the night before, skipped lunch to get a project finished and worked all day without real breaks. When our body gets low on energy due to lack of sleep or oxygen, or low blood sugar levels, both our body and brain go into power save mode.

When your smart phone goes below a certain battery charge, you probably get a notification asking if you want to go to power save mode. When our brain (which uses approximately 20% of our total energy) starts to lack energy, it too goes into power save mode – we just don't get such a clear notification.

When our brain starts prioritising energy resources, it won't power down the deeper parts of our brain controlling body functions such as heart rate, breathing, etc. Activity in the limbic system, including the amygdala, normally continues at the same level as before as these functions are crucial for our survival. What powers down first when we are low on energy is the typically the upper parts of the brain, like our prefrontal cortex. With the parts of our brain responsible for regulating emotional impulses from the amygdala and the limbic system being on 'power save mode', we are much more likely to become the victim of our own emotions.

We have probably all witnessed the result of this in ourselves and others. When we are 'low on battery' we are more likely to get emotional, irritated and impulsive. It is not that we are bad people, it is just that our brain struggles to operate at its full potential. The business case for using some of the tools and principles we explore in Chapter 1 on Sustainable High Performance, for example, building micro-pauses into your workday, is that it enables our brain to work better. So, if you want to maintain a balanced mind throughout your day, it can be worth keeping track of your energy levels and developing habits that help you recharge when you need to.

## STOP to create a moment of choice

Even when we are well rested and feel energised, we can still get derailed at times and lose our mental balance. As we have explored in the chapters on self-awareness, we all have certain situations that tend to trigger us, where we easily get hi-jacked by our emotions or go into our habitual autopilot behaviors. To create the mental space we need to make more conscious choices in these situations, it helps to have a very concrete practice to apply when emotions starts to rise.

The STOP practice explained below is such a tool. It builds on things most of us know intuitively but may not be able to practice when we are under pressure. STOP is an acronym for:

- Stop chain-reaction
- Take deep breaths
- Observe emotions and thoughts
- Proceed in the most helpful way

The STOP practice is largely common sense, put on a formula. But as they say, common sense is not always common practice. We will now walk through the different steps in the STOP practice to give you a sense of the key points of each step, as well as the neuroscientific perspective to what happens in our brain when we apply them.

### Stopping the chain-reaction

When we get an emotional reaction, a biochemical chain-reaction starts in our brain and body. It is this chain-reaction that triggers autopilot behaviors and can lead to us say or doing things we will regret later.

But how long does this bio-chemical reaction last? Think about it – for how long can you be irritated? The answer probable ranges from minutes to days... From a purely biological perspective, we can actually not have an emotional reaction for very long. Research indicates that the biochemicals related to feeling, for example, anger only stays in our system for about 90 seconds. So how can we be angry for so long?

What happens when we maintain an emotional state for longer than 90 seconds is that we keep nourishing the reactions with our thoughts. We keep focusing on that thing that triggers us, which makes us play repeat on those 90 seconds over and over again. Hence, we can be angry or irritated for a very long time.

The good news in this is that if we are able to move our attention away from whatever initially triggered us, the biochemical chain-reaction will slow down and fade out within a few seconds. This is why the classical advice; 'if you get upset, count to 10', actually works. We can find and develop our own version of a technique like 'counting to 10', as long as it helps us remove our focus from the triggering thought or event, if only for a few seconds.

From experience, most of us know that it isn't that easy to move our attention away from something that has triggered us, once we are starting to get upset. It isn't easy, but it can actually be practiced. This brings us back to one of the side-benefits of attention training or mindfulness practice that we introduced in Chapter 1. Numerous research studies have shown that people who have a regular mindfulness practice seem to regulate their own emotional reactions more easily. If we look at the mechanics of mindfulness practice, this makes sense. When we practice mindfulness, we train our ability to notice when our focus wanders off, and deliberately place our attention on something neutral like the breath. With regular mindfulness practice, we strengthen the mental muscle that helps us control our attention, hence it also makes us better at harnessing it when are getting caught up in an emotional reaction.

### Taking deep breaths

The T in the STOP formula is closely related to stopping the chain-reaction. When moving our attention away from the triggering event, we can place it on something neutral that we always have with us – our breath.

Again, you have heard this since you were a kid; 'take a deep breath to calm down'. Besides helping us move our focus away from whatever triggers us, it also has a biological benefit. Slow and deep breathing stimulates our vagus nerve as we covered earlier and helps us calm down our nervous system. Just a few deep, slow breaths can be enough to create the mental space we need to center ourselves again.

As a supplement to focusing on your breath, we can also use our body as an anchor for our attention. Feeling our feet on the floor or our body sitting in the chair can help us feel more grounded.

The first two elements, S and T of the STOP practice, are aimed at dampening the emotional override in our brain and give our more rational pre-frontal cortex a chance to come on-line again. This, in turn, gives us the ability to more objectively take in what is happening.

### Observing the situation

With O for observing, we try to put some perspectives on the situation. Like a journalist observing an event to report it correctly, we notice for ourselves what is going on. There are different sources of data we can take in here:

#### Observing our emotions

As we have explored earlier, we can put a little distance between ourselves and our emotions by observing and labeling the emotions present in us at that moment. The more we familiarise ourselves with our different emotions and how they express themselves through our self-awareness practices, the easier this will be.

To create a more objective relation to any emotional reaction, it often helps to notice the physical sensation itself. Instead of labeling yourself as 'being angry', you can focus on the pure sensation, like 'I notice tension in my jaws'.

By not identifying with a certain emotion but rather labeling the physical sensation you are observing, you are creating some space between yourself and the emotional reaction.

#### Observing your thoughts

Our mind is a storytelling machine, and especially when we get emotional, all kinds of narratives spin out about what is happening. Just like with observing our emotional reactions as objectively as possible, we can also take an objective view on the thoughts that well up in the given situation.

Notice what thoughts are dominating in your mind, and what story you are telling yourself about the other people involved, about yourself or what is going to happen next. If you can step out of your narrative for a moment and see it from the outside, you can reality check if the story your mind is spinning at that moment is really true.

### Getting perspectives

If you are able to do the previous mental moves, you are well on your way to getting more perspectives on the situation. You can compare this to being at a sports game, but instead of being on the playing field fighting for the ball, you are sitting in the audience watching the game. We all know it is easier to get the overview from that perspective.

A part of getting perspectives is to reflect on patterns. What can you recognise from similar situations. Are there other situations where the same things play out and you react the same way?

If you are able to really step out of you own position for a moment, you may also want to take the perspectives of the other people involved. What might be reasons for why they are acting the way they are? You do not have to agree with their point of view, just be curious about what might drive their behavior.

### Proceeding in the most helpful way

From the perspective of the objective observer, we can then move to P for proceed.

In this position, we reflect on what options we have. We can acknowledge that our usual autopilot behavior might still be an option, but here we give ourselves a moment to consider what potential other actions we could take. What would be the most skillful way to handle the situation? What would have the best long-term effect? There might not be a perfect option, but by going through the steps of STOP, we are likely to have created enough mental space to take a more conscious decision.

If we can apply the four steps of the STOP practice in situations when we feel stressed or start to get upset, it can help us create some mental space to act more wisely. However, to remember to do this often requires some practice. In the next section, we will explore a method for priming our mind and prepare for challenging situations.

## Using the STOP practice in preparing for difficult situations

The STOP practice is a very concrete tool to be used in all kinds of situations where you need to take conscious action. As mentioned earlier, the four steps are pretty common sense. However, just knowing intellectually that this practice can be helpful, doesn't mean that you are able to use it in difficult situations.

Let us imagine for a moment that you are not very good at swimming. However, you have read a book about swimming with some excellent tips for how to do it. If shortly thereafter, you happen to fall into the water, to what extent will it help you that you had read the book? The benefit would, of course, be marginal.

However, if you invested the time to go to a swimming pool and try out the techniques in a safe environment, you would probably build sufficient skill over time, and be more capable of handling the situation if you were to fall into the water again.

It is a bit like in the old Karate Kid movie from the 1980s (if you are in certain age group you will know what I refer to...). Daniel-San did the 'wax on, wax off' and 'sand the floor' many times before he had learned the moves so well, he could actually apply them in a martial arts context.

Mental capabilities, like attention or emotional regulation, are not that different from physical skills. They too develop best through practice. A good thing about growing our mental ability to cope with difficult situations is that we can actually practice it without 'falling into the water', i.e. being in the difficult situation itself.

You have probably heard about elite athletes doing various forms of mental training to prepare themselves for top performance. One of these training techniques is visualisation, where the athletes see themselves doing, for example, the perfect penalty shoot, high jump, or other key moment of performance. Athletes do this well in advance of the game, to prime their mind toward optimal performance in the moment of truth.

In the same way, we can prepare ourselves for the moments where we know we might be challenged, by visualising the scenario, and mentally walk through how we could handle it skilfully. Below is a guided exercise you can use to practice the moves of STOP in a safe space, and through that mentally prepare yourself for difficult situations.

### Visualisation – rehearsing for a difficult scenario

Think about a concrete scenario where you know there is a risk that you will 'go on autopilot' and not necessarily handle the situation in the best possible way. Please choose a situation that is likely to occur again, and where you feel it would be valuable if you could handle it differently from how you normally do.

- *Find a place where you can be undisturbed for around ten minutes.*
- *Take a comfortable seat and close your eyes. Take a few deep breaths to settle in.*
- *Bring your case scenario to mind. Allow yourself to mentally go into the situation and imagine it in all details. Where are you? Who is there? What is happening? Who is saying what?*

- *As you are visualising this, you may start noticing emotions and even physiological sensations showing up in your body. This would be your early warning sign that you are reacting emotionally to the situation. If that doesn't show up in this exercise, just imagine yourself in the real scenario – what would be your early warnings signs there? How will you know that you have started to react and run the risk of derailing?*
- *When you have identified your early warning, this is the moment to apply STOP.*
- *Start with taking a few really deep and slow breaths. As you do that, feel the air coming in and out. Feel your body sitting well-grounded in the chair and your feet steadily planted on the floor.*
- *Once you have grounded your attention, start observing your emotions and thoughts. If you experience emotions even as you do the visualisation, you can observe these in your body. If not, just picture yourself in the future scenario; what emotions and thoughts are likely to show up?*
- *To help you see them clearly and a bit objectively, try putting names or labels to the thoughts and emotions you are experiencing.*
- *Now, reflect on your options. What alternatives do you have for how to act in this situation?*
- *See yourself doing what you discern to be the most skillful move.*
- *How does it feel?*
- *Imagine for yourself what the response might be from the other people involved.*
- *Sit with this outcome in your mind for a moment before you wrap up the exercise.*
- *Finish with a few deep breaths, and slowly come out of the exercise.*

This kind of mental role play is a way of priming your mind for the next time you encounter a similar situation in real life. There is nothing magical about it, you have just created some new neural pathways, so the next time you are in that situation, it is likely that a part of your mind will remind you that you have options for how to respond.

Just like athletes, we can practice priming our mind to increase the chances that we show up the way we would like to do in important situations. Spending a few minutes like this preparing for a potentially challenging situation can be a worthwhile investment. I could help you create what Victor Frankl called "the space between stimuli and response" that enables you to handle the situation more skilfully.

## Learning to observe our own mind – the next level of mindfulness practice

In the last sections, we have explored different ways to cultivate our self-awareness, regulate our emotional states and apply more conscious action. In a sense, we have covered different ways of acting more mindfully. It might therefore be relevant to revisit a topic we worked with earlier in the book – the practice of mindfulness meditation.

In Chapter 1, we looked at mindfulness meditation from the perspective of reducing stress and strengthening our ability to be focused. However, there is a wider scope to mindfulness practice that is relevant for enhancing self-awareness as well as self-leadership.

Much of our mental activity is repetitive and automated, which can be useful in many contexts. But not all habitual mental activity is helpful. As you probably have noticed, our mind can ruminate or create stories on its own without any relation to reality. As we touched on before, it can therefore be useful to cultivate our ability to observe our thoughts and emotions objectively, to discern more clearly what of our mental activity is relevant and not. The next level of mindfulness meditation practice is about learning to observe our own mind, thought processes and emotions with clarity and curiosity.

If we look at the meaning of the words for 'meditation' in old languages like Pali and Sanskrit, it will translate to 'getting familiar with' and 'cultivating'. Long before modern psychology and neuroscience, meditation was a technique used to understand and cultivate our own minds. In addition to practicing our ability to focus, mindfulness meditation also entails observing and getting to know our own mental processes.

### Mindfulness of thoughts and emotions

In our earlier mindfulness practice, we trained our attention muscle by having our breath at the center of our attention and returning to it every time our mind wandered.

When practicing mindfulness of thoughts and emotions, we let these mental processes be objects for our attention. The practice follows the same basic structure as when focusing on our breath, and we still use our breath as an anchor when our mind starts wandering off. But instead of just focusing on our breath, we widen the scope and make observing thoughts, images and emotions a part of the practice.

The key training element here is to observe without engaging. When thoughts or images show up in your mind, you just watch them without doing anything with them. If you start engaging with a thought, a narrative starts building and a moment later you will find yourself lost in a trail of thoughts, one leading to the other. But if you can just observe, you will notice that every thought that shows up quickly fades away and is replaced by a new one. The key in this practice is to learn to let go, again and again, and come back to a place of neutral observing.

Here are some basic principles for how you can practice mindfulness of thoughts and emotions:

- *Find a place where you can be undisturbed and set a timer for the number of minutes you would like to practice.*
- *Find a comfortable position where you feel relaxed and still alert.*
- *Start with taking a few deep breaths, and then let your breathing fall into a natural rhythm without you interfering with it. Just let your attention rest on the sensation of breathing.*
- *When images, thoughts or emotions show up, notice them with curiosity. You don't have to engage with them, just simply label them 'thinking', or 'emotion' and let them be. After a moment they will fade away or morph into something else. Just keep observing.*
- *If you find yourself getting entangled with a thought or emotion, don't worry about it. Just gently return your attention to your breath to anchor yourself in an observing position again. Relax, and watch as the next thought, image or emotion arise and leave again.*

Watching our thoughts come and go without immediately engaging with them trains our ability to have a more relaxed relationship to all the activity in our mind. We experience directly that we don't have to struggle so much with the never-ending inner stream of thoughts, images and emotions. By practicing to observe and let go, we create a healthy distance to our mental chatter and can be less ruled by it.

This mental 'gym practice' supports many of the previous applications related to self-awareness and self-leadership. When we on a regular basis train ourselves to notice thoughts and emotions as they show up and not immediately identify with them, we strengthen our ability to pause our autopilots and act more consciously in everyday situations.

## Working with awareness-based change

*The definition of insanity is to keep doing the same thing as before, expecting a new result*

Quote attributed to Albert Einstein

Any kind of change or transformation, may it be on a personal or organisational level, entails that we need to start doing some things differently from before. Given what we have explored in this book, we know that our evolutionary programming actually makes it rather difficult for us to change behaviors. We are to a large degree hard-wired to repeat habitual behaviors, and it takes conscious effort to change.

I once attended a keynote with Jeremy Hunter,[7] a professor of practice at the Peter Drucker school of management, who teaches MBA students on self-leadership. Hunter spoke about the gap between having good intentions and really creating new results. He pointed to the fact that to close that gap between intentions and results, we must first become aware of our habits, and identify the situations where we can make conscious choices to try new behaviors.

Inspired by Jeremy Hunter's principles, I have found the ladder below to be a helpful visualisation for what it takes to succeed with any kind of change of transformation.

### Intention

In Alice in Wonderland, Alice asks the Cat what way she should go. The Cat asks Alice where she is heading. "I don't know", says Alice. "Then it doesn't matter which way you are going", the Cat replies.

Having a clear intention is, of course, the starting point of any change effort. Sometimes it takes some work to define what you really want to accomplish, what good looks like, and how you will know when you are there.

But setting the intention is often the easy part. The following steps are what enable it to become real.

### Attention

Based on your intention, what are the important interactions and 'moments of truth' you must pay attention to that will determine if your intention will come true or not?

INTENTION
↓
ATTENTION
↓
AWARENESS
↓
MOMENT OF CHOICE
↓
NEW BEHAVIOR
↓
NEW RESULT

*Figure 2.2* **The six steps from good intentions to new results.**

Let us say that you want to improve inclusion in your team and involve your team members more actively in decision making. You have therefore set an intention to be less dominating and listen more to other's input.

To move toward that goal, you have to start paying close *attention* to how you are actually behaving in for example team meetings.

### Awareness

By homing in your attention, you will start noticing the current patterns more clearly. You will become more *aware* of group dynamics and how your own behaviors influence others. You will notice both positive things as well as behaviors that need adjusting.

If your intention is to create more inclusion, you might, for example, become aware of that you are pretty good at involving your team members by asking questions, but maybe also that you have a tendency to answer your own questions if others don't come up with the 'right answer' quick enough...

### Moment of choice

Attention and awareness are the first keys to change. Until you start seeing the patterns and behaviors, they will be blind spots, and you will not make much progress despite the best intention. But once you become aware of the patterns, you have a choice. You can pause yourself in the moment of truth and try acting differently.

As we have explored earlier relating to conscious action and how to turn off the autopilot, you can now work with the STOP practice, or any other method, to create enough mental space in the moment for you to reflect on how you should act.

### New behavior

The next step is experimenting with doing something different from before. Changing our habits is never easy, and trying out a new behavior will often feel uncomfortable. The key thing in this step is to really reflect on what options you have. There may not be one right answer for how to act, and you may have to experiment with different ways.

Sometimes it can be a powerful thing to share your intentions with the people affected by it, including what new behaviors you are trying to implement. Thereby you can get their support and feedback on how you are developing.

### New results

When you act differently, it will influence your environment in one way or another. If you have set an intention with a clear idea of what you want to accomplish, you can evaluate if your new behavior leads to the result you intended, or if you will need to keep adjusting and experimenting.

The essence of this simple six-step model is that at the core of any change or transformation lies our ability to be really mindful. To pay close attention and become aware of what is really going on. The awareness opens for new choices, conscious action, and potentially new results.

No matter what change or transformation you want to succeed with, you can try reflecting on the six steps, how they apply to your situation, and if there are some of the steps you want to focus more on.

## Building our self-leadership step by step

In this chapter, we have explored how we can stay smart under pressure and live in line with our values, aspirations and intentions, also when we are experiencing challenging situations. There are no silver bullets offered here, just research-based methods and practices that have been shown to work, if we apply them with some level of consistency.

Whatever habits we have, they often exist because they have served us before, one way or the other. Adjusting these habits takes time and some work. It is a slow but interesting process to close the gap between what we know and what we do.

As a way to summarise what we have covered, we can look at our ability to lead ourselves as being developed in steps over time. You can use the

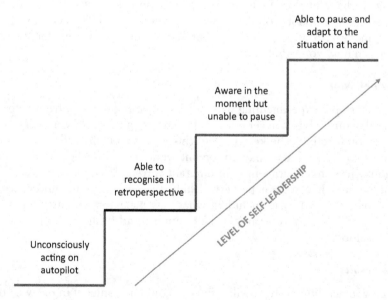

*Figure 2.3* Building our self-leadership step by step.

steps described here to reflect on how you are relating to various situations in your life. Most likely you are at different levels of self-leadership in relation to different situations.

### Unconsciously on autopilot

Without engaging in some kind of self-reflection and honest examination, we risk being stuck in autopilot. Some of our habitual behaviors serve us, and some not.

To develop ourselves, as individuals, organisations or as a society, often starts a curious inquiry, where we dare to look at our behaviors and what the effects they have.

The journey of growing self-awareness often takes some courage and should therefore be accompanied by self-compassion. We can often use some help from the outside, like feedback from a trusted friend or a 360-degree survey providing us with some perspectives on how others perceive us.

With an open mind and open heart, we can acknowledge what works well and what doesn't, and take the first step toward self-leadership.

### Retrospectively aware

It can be difficult to notice our own behaviors clearly in real time. The first step in self-awareness is usually to be able to reflect on situations in retrospect and consider what has been helpful and how we would like to handle things differently in the future.

Our brain has a negativity bias, hence we tend to focus more on what went wrong than what we did well. However, there is as much learning in becoming aware of our strengths as well, so we can leverage them even better in the future.

For the parts that need development, it is important to look at ourselves honestly but with 'soft eyes'. The more we can take a compassionate stance, the more we can typically acknowledge our shortcomings and be willing to work with them.

Once we have started to become aware about what we would like to do differently, if only in retrospect, we can take responsibility for our future actions. We have opened a door to new possibilities. We can reflect on what options we have the next time a similar situation occurs, and we can even prime our mind by visualising how we want to act in future scenarios.

### Aware, but unable to pause

The next stage in self-leadership is when we start noticing in real time how we go into autopilot behavior. But it can still be difficult to break out of the habitual behavior. We can, for example, notice how we are getting upset in a given situation and say things we know are not helpful.

This can be very frustrating, and it is easy to beat ourselves up for 'doing it again…'. But noticing in the moment, is an important step toward self-leadership. By becoming aware of what is happening in real time, we can collect valuable data on what triggers us and how we act our own patterns out. This, in turn, opens for the next stage.

### Aware and able to call it out

As we covered earlier, a key to development in ourselves and our organisations, is creating awareness. Once we start to see triggers and patterns clearly, we have the possibility to call it out.

We might not be able to stop ourselves from reacting, but we can be transparent and put words to it. It can make a world of difference in a meeting if a person is able to say "I notice that this subject makes me uncomfortable. I just want to be open with that if you notice me getting a bit defensive here".

Sometimes we don't want to share what we notice at that moment, but we can choose to do it afterwards. If we have had a difficult meeting, we might want to follow up with the people involved, take responsibility for our contribution to the situation and share what we have noticed about ourselves.

This does not mean that we should always pour our feelings out or take everything on ourselves. We must discern what is ours to take responsibility for and what is relevant to share. However, few things earn people as much respect as having the courage to admit their shortcomings and taking responsibility for them.

### Able to pause and adapt

Over time, we can come to a point where we are able to notice our early warning signs even in challenging situations, pause our habitual reactions and make more conscious choices on how to act. This is the essence of (self) leadership as we have explored it. The ability to sense what the given situation calls for and adapt our response to support the best possible outcome.

It would be utopian to think we can do this in all kinds of situations. There will always be certain scenarios that bring us more out of balance than others. But, by building our self-leadership step by step we can learn how to stay smart under pressure, be less ruled by circumstances and more able to show up as the version of ourselves we would like to be.

These capabilities also come in handy and lay the foundation for what we will explore in the coming chapter – how to navigate skilfully in change and complexity.

## Notes

1 See more in Robert Sapolsky's keynote speech at Stanford University in 2017. Search for: *Robert Sapolsky – The Biology of Humans at Our Best and Worst*.
2 To watch Jim Tamm's TED Talk about early warning signs, search for: *Cultivating Collaboration: Don't Be So Defensive! – Jim Tamm – TEDxSantaCruz*. He has also written the book *Radical Collaboration: Five Essential Skills to Overcome Defensiveness and Build Successful Relationships* (2004).
3 Nummenmaa et al., 2013. researchgate.net/publication/259499731_Bodily_maps_of_emotions.
4 J. Smyth, *Written Emotional Expression: Effect Sizes, Outcome Types, and Moderating Variables* (1998). pure.psu.edu/en/publications/written-emotional-expression-effect-sizes-outcome-types-and-moder
5 Search Inside Yourself started as an internal program at Google in 2007 for training emotional intelligence in leaders and engineers. Grounded in neuroscience and using mindfulness practices, the program became a success, and since 2012 the program is being offered outside of Google through a non-profit organisation called Search Inside Yourself Leadership Institute (SIYLI). You can read more about the background, research, and trainings on siyli.org and siyglobal.com. I can also recommend the light-hearted and practical book by the one of the founders of the program, Chade-Meng Tan, *Search Inside Yourself* (2012).
6 Victor E. Frankl, *Man's Search for Meaning* (1959).
7 You can read more about Jeremy Hunter and find examples of his work on cgu.edu/people/jeremy-hunter.

# Chapter 3

# Navigating skilfully in change, uncertainty and complexity

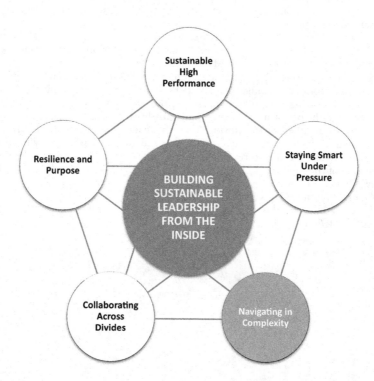

*Figure 3.1* The five areas of building sustainable leadership from the inside.

**Overview Chapter 3: Navigating skilfully in change, uncertainty and complexity**

Many of us are well trained in working with complicated problems where we can apply a clear process and work ourselves toward a

DOI: 10.4324/9781003485148-4

solution in a structured way. But the messiness and uncertainty that comes with transformations or truly complex challenges can be discomforting and frustrating.

In this chapter, we explore mental capabilities we can cultivate to navigate more skilfully in complex situations. We will build on some capabilities covered in previous chapters, and add practices related to understanding mental models, system dynamics and how to combine analytical thinking with our ability for intuitive intelligence.

*These are some of the areas we are going to cover:*

- The difference between complicated and complex problems and how they require different cognitive approaches
- An overview of personal capabilities that help us navigate in complexity
- The idea of negative capability and our ability to be comfortable with creative tension
- Using self-compassion to nurture a learning mindset
- Creating awareness of our mental models, assumptions and limiting beliefs
- The ladder of inference and practicing clear perception
- Understanding systems and their underlying structures
- Practicing our levels of listening
- Using envisioning to prime our brain and guide our mind
- The idea of emergence
- Understanding intuitive intelligence and how to leverage it wisely

*Examples of how this part relates to and supports other sections:*

- The openness and curiosity needed to navigate complexity links to elements around self-leadership in *Staying Smart Under Pressure* as well as empathy and compassion covered in *Collaborating across Divides*.
- We leverage the sections related to self-awareness and self-compassion introduced in *Staying Smart Under Pressure* and introduce deeper practices in these areas.
- The way we approach methods for increasing our systems awareness in this part also links to the final part of the book around *Resilience and Purpose*.

*Supporting audio material:*
There are guided audio practices accompanying this chapter. Search for *Meditations for Leaders (Joakim Eriksson)* to find them on your preferred audio platform.

## Impermanence and uncertainty as a part of life

Change and uncertainty is an inevitable part of life, but that doesn't mean it is easy to cope with it. You have probably had your own share of experiences with messy changes in your professional and personal life and lived through the period of uncertainty and frustration that comes with it.

Sometimes things are stirred up close to us, for example, through a larger change in the organisation we are working for. But even when things in our proximity are operating as usual, there are probably changes going on in our society, political environment or market conditions, requiring us to respond or think differently about things.

Many years ago, the term VUCA (Volatility, Uncertainty, Complexity, Ambiguity) was introduced in the military to describe the new and often unpredictable conditions facing decision makers. Since then, another term, BANI (Brittle, Anxious, Non-linear, Incomprehensible), has been introduced, pointing to some of the dynamics present in our current global society.

No matter where we are working, may it be in the arena of global politics or trying to virtually lead a team of geographically spread colleagues, we all have our own examples of working with complex and ambiguous situations.

Although there are many theories and models for how to lead an organisation in change and complexity, few address how we can lead ourselves in these circumstances. In this chapter, we will therefore explore some of the inner aspects of change and transformation, and how we through training can learn to navigate more skilfully in the discomfort of uncertainty.

## The character of complex and wicked problems

Before we start exploring personal practices, it may be relevant to set the frame by looking at what typically characterises complex challenges. My aspiration here is not to provide a full definition, but just point to why and how the personal capabilities we will look at later are relevant.

### Complicated or complex

In daily life, we might use these words interchangeably, but for the sake of our exploration, let us look at how they point to different characteristics of a problem.

To use examples, a computer or a mechanical watch can be said to be complicated. They both consist of a large number of parts that are put together to create a working machine. If we encounter a problem with our watch or computer, most of us cannot just open the lid and fix it. It takes knowledge, methodology, and training to be able to be able solve complicated problems; to take things apart, diagnose the problem and fix the broken part.

But, with sufficient training and experience, a watch maker or IT engineer can do this with predictable results. And once the broken part is fixed, we can trust that the watch or computer will work again.

A complex problem, however, is better compared with a weather pattern or a traffic jam. As with a watch or a computer, there are many interacting elements, but they don't work together in a linear or mechanical way. Rather, the different elements influence each other in unpredictable ways, which make it very difficult to analyse and foresee what is going to happen. This is why despite all the technology and well-trained meteorologists we have in the world, we can never know for sure what the weather is going to be tomorrow. And when there is a messy traffic jam, it is rather impossible to isolate and define the one thing we could do to fix it.

A complex problem is often described as being characterised by a multitude of independent elements (for example, macroeconomics, organisational culture, interpersonal dynamics, etc.), interacting in ways that seem unpredictable. Hence, there are no given solutions we can trust based on previous experiences, and we cannot search for the one right answer on the internet or in a textbook. Instead, we must apply patience and curiosity, exploring the problem, looking for the underlying patterns that can give us a clue to how to move forward.

This is where it is interesting to look at the personal capabilities required to navigate skilfully in complex situations. If we as individuals for example get frustrated and rigid or try to 'beat' a complex problem by trying to intellectually understand all the details, we are likely to get stuck. Our cognitive capabilities for analysing and planning are excellent for solving complicated problems, but for the complex ones, we may need to supplement with other skills and abilities, which we will explore further down.

## Approaching complexity and uncertainty

If you are curious to learn more about how to understand and work with complex problems, one of the leading figures in the field has been the organisational theorist Ralph Stacey[1] whose large body of work has inspired many others. Another tip is to check out Dave Snowden,[2] the creator of the Cynefin Framework, a helpful tool for making sense of complex challenges.

Stacey, Snowden, and many others have provided guidance for how to think about and approach complex challenges and situations where uncertainty is high. They typically point to the importance of:

- Being responsive to shifting circumstances
- Patience and capacity to stay with our uncertainty

- Vulnerability and openness to what we don't know
- Curiosity and willingness to explore different perspectives
- Creating space for reflection and sensing emerging patterns

In organisational development and leadership, there are processes and tools you can apply to support this way of working. Agile project management being one of many examples. What we are going to focus on in this chapter however, are what personal skills and capabilities we can cultivate, to be able to use these processes and tools effectively.

## Perspectives on using our whole brain

You may have heard about the idea that the left and right hemispheres of our brain represent different characteristics of mental functions. However, researchers are today reluctant to associate certain traits and abilities with one of the hemispheres only. Studies using brain scans have not been able to find evidence of dominating left/right side activity correlating with personality traits, certain cognitive capabilities, etc.

The notion of some people being more left-brained or right-brained should be seen more as a figure of speech than an anatomically accurate description. There is still a consensus, however, that our brains have certain 'modes' which represent very different mental functions.

The so-called left-brain mode is often attributed to things as:

- Analysis, facts, and logic
- Concepts, words, and language
- Cause and effect, and linear thinking

According to the same theory, the so-called right-brain mode is more related to:

- Metaphors, stories, and social interaction
- Nonverbal communication, emotions, and bodily awareness
- Holistic thinking and intuition

The left or right brain mode can be more or less developed in us, based on genetical disposition, life experiences and how we have used our brain throughout our life. We use both modes to navigate in life, but one mode with its associated functions can be dominating. Most personality profile assessments will give us an indication of our preferred style.

According to Dan Siegel,[3] professor in psychology at UCLA, author of *Mindsight*[4] and many other books, the left and right brain modes represent different ways of relating to the world. Where the left-brain mode deals more in absolutes; "Is X or Y the answer?", the right-brain mode is more oriented around patterns and connections. "How can X and Y be related and relevant in different contexts?" How we use these modes becomes relevant in relation to working with complicated vs. complex problems.

The characteristic of our left-brain mode serves us well when approaching a complicated challenge. Its analytical, linear, cause-and-effect orientation helps us structure a problem and work toward the right solution. The non-linearity and unpredictability of a complex challenge, however, often calls for a more holistic approach where we must look for the patterns beyond the details.

One of the key functions of the right-brain mode is accessing and regulating information coming from our subcortical regions, such as our limbic system, brain stem and the neural centers distributed throughout our body. As we will explore more later, the subcortical regions process vast amounts of data points from social interactions, our surroundings as well as our body, to help us sense emerging patterns. We often experience the result of this subconscious processing as a vague sense, a hunch or a 'gut feeling'. This, as we can refer to as a more intuitive intelligence, can be very useful when navigating in complexity and uncertainty.

Our ability for pattern recognition and intuition is linked to how we use other aspects of the right-brain mode, such as visualisation, attention to feelings, emotions as well as bodily sensations. Siegel's research and long clinical experience indicates that we can stimulate and develop our right-brain mode by cultivating these various functions.

Navigating the various situations we face in life requires a fluid integration of both left- and right-brain functions. If we sense that our personality leans more to left-brain activation, we can deliberately work on integrating right-brain activities, so we can meet challenges with a whole brain approach.

## Four personal skills and capabilities for navigating complexity and uncertainty

In the following sections, we are going to look at four different areas we can cultivate to strengthen our personal capabilities for navigating complexity and uncertainty. The practices related to these areas support right-brain mode activation and left/right integration.

The four areas are:

### Openness and relaxation

When we experience uncertainty, a natural reaction for our brain is to go into threat response, which shuts down our ability for big picture thinking and limits our ability to take in new information. By noticing early

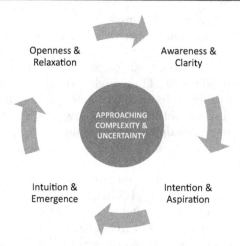

*Figure 3.2* Skills for approaching complexity.

warnings signs, like thoughts and emotions indicating we are getting anxious or rigid, we can train ourselves to relax into the current circumstances, and deliberately cultivate an open and curious approach.

### Awareness and clear seeing

To understand and navigate complex situations, we need to pay close attention to what is happening beyond obvious events. This level of awareness includes being curious about the deeper dynamics and underlying structures in a situation, as well as being aware of our own biases and mental models that might influence and limit our understanding.

### Intention and aspirations

In complex situations, it can often be difficult to set clear goals or make comprehensive action plans. However, we can work with clear intentions and long-term aspirations, and use these to give us a sense of direction through uncertainty.

### Intuition and emergence

The deeper, subcortical parts of our brain have an enormous capacity for recognising patterns in data and making connections between seemingly unrelated pieces of information. We can learn to tap into this resource of creativity and leverage it when facing complex situations and wicked problems.

## Cultivating relaxation and openness

### We are hardwired to react to uncertainty

From an evolutionary perspective, predictability has been better for our survival than uncertainty. Even if we in our modern societies are expected to be adaptable and open to change, our ancient neurological programming still prefers to know what happens next.

David Rock[5] has written a practical and insightful book called *Your Brain at Work*,[6] where he explains many of the psychological dynamics we can recognise in our work life, through the lens of evolution and neuroscience. One of the key models Rock introduces is the SCARF model, which points to five themes that have been important to our survival through evolution:

* Status
* Certainty
* Autonomy
* Relatedness
* Fairness

Our mind is constantly scanning our environment and will react if something changes for the better or worse in any of these areas. For example, a situation that we perceive as positive to our sense of *status* would trigger a reward response in our brain. On the contrary, experiencing *unfair* treatment, loss of *autonomy* or increased *uncertainty* would often trigger a threat response.

Objectively, most of us live a very safe and comfortable life, compared to our ancestors. Despite that, we can experience overwhelming feelings, stress and even a sense of being threatened from time to time. Although we are not physically threatened, our nervous system can still go into survival mode.

The SCARF model is a simple but helpful guide to understanding and even predicting our own and other's reactions to things that happen. As you can see, there are many themes in the SCARF model that are likely to be triggered when we are facing a complex problem or a difficult transformation. Understanding that these reactions are natural and evolutionary programmed can help us see them more clearly and not be so hi-jacked by them.

### The idea of negative capability

As we covered in the previous sections, it is totally normal to feel uncomfortable when facing change and uncertainty. However, to navigate skilfully in a complex and ever-changing world, we must learn to deal with that sense of discomfort without becoming reactive.

There is an interesting term in psychology that refers to this skill called *negative capability*, i.e. the ability to be with negative experiences without being overwhelmed by them. The term is said to originate from the romantic poet John Keats in the 19th century. Keats used the term to describe the ability of an artist to be in confusion and uncertainty without immediately reaching for absolute answers or solutions that relied on established norms. Keats argued that this *negative capability* was a core trait of great writers like Shakespeare and others, who had been able to create work that reached beyond what was the norms of the time.

Even if we don't see ourselves as writers or artists, there are many parallels between what Keats once described and the challenges leaders in our complex world face. We too are called to be creative and find solutions to wicked problems without being able to rely on established norms or textbook answers.

Peter Senge, a well-known systems thinker, and researcher in the field of learning organisations, talks about *creative tension*. In the gap between our aspirations (how we would like things to be) and current reality, there is this natural tension. This tension can be the driver for creativity and change, but the gap can also be experienced as uncomfortable and frustrating. Senge points to that if we cannot be with the creative tension, we tend to either lower our aspirations or try to tell ourselves that our current reality is better than it is. That way the gap gets smaller, and we feel less discomfort. However, Senge further argues that to drive necessary transformations, may it be in our personal lives, our organisation or in society, we must be able to be with the discomfort and hold the creative tension.

This so-called negative capability is an innate trait for all of us, but it can be enhanced by many of the principles and practices we have explored in previous chapters, especially around self-awareness and self-leadership. Developing our early warning system and a clear understanding of how we typically react when we get uncertain or uncomfortable can help us pause and reflect instead of becoming reactive. By applying the STOP practice we can refrain from going into autopilot behaviors to relieve our frustration, and instead stay curious and mindful.

Training ourselves to tolerate feelings of discomfort and uncertainty, without knee-jerking with our habitual reactions, gives us a larger freedom of action. In the following sections, we will explore a few approaches to how we can do this.

### From anxiety and rigidity to openness and learning

In one of the first chapters, we looked at how activation of the sympathetic and parasympathetic influences what hormones go out in our body as well as what functions in our brain get most activated.

When we perceive change and uncertainty as a threat, our nervous system goes into self-protection mode and releases adrenalin and cortisol. Although this can make us focused and action oriented, it also shuts down much of our big picture thinking and creativity. In this neural mode, we tend to be pretty short sighted and cling to behaviors that have worked for us before.

However, if we interpret the situation as a learning scenario, our brain releases dopamine. We are more motivated to explore new solutions and to collaborate with others.

Amy Edmondson,[7] a professor at Harvard Business School, has been a leading researcher on psychological safety in organisations and how that influences efficiency and innovation. In her book *The Fearless Organization*[8] she unpacks the relation between psychological safety and high performance. Edmondson argues that the combination of expectations of high standards, combined with a psychologically safe environment creates a culture of learning.

In these kinds of organisations, aspirations are high, and people are focused on performance and development. What makes people willing to lean in to difficult and complex problems, is the atmosphere and experience that they have each other's backs. Psychological safety is sometimes described as the sense that my colleagues will support and help me if I make a mistake, not beat me up for it. That sense of safety and support makes people relax, their brains work better, and they can be more creative together.

### Self-compassion as a prerequisite for a learning mindset

There is a large body of research suggesting that teams and organisations that have high psychological safety are more innovative and better at tackling complex problems. The equivalent of psychological safety on a personal level is self-compassion, which we have touched on earlier.

At the core of self-compassion is the principle of being kind and supportive of ourselves, even when we make mistakes. This does not mean having no expectations of ourselves. To draw a parallel to Edmondson's framework for high performing and learning organisation, self-compassion includes both holding ourselves to high standards and accepting the fact that it is human to fail.

Just as a supportive and trusting atmosphere in your team at work can help you feel relaxed and open, so does applying a self-compassionate attitude toward yourself. The research of Kristin Neff, Chris Germer as well as Serena Chen[9] suggests that people who actively work with self-compassion are more creative and braver when it comes to exploring new ways of working.

If we tend to be hard on ourselves and expect perfection, our response to a difficult and complex situation will probably be fear-based. We put an unspoken expectation on ourselves to 'get it right' which is a tough if not impossible task when facing a complex problem. With this attitude toward ourselves there is a risk that our mind cramps rather than being creative. A fear-based mind tends to ruminate about what has or could go wrong, which is an evolutionary function. As neuroscientist and evolutionary psychologist Rick Hanson[10] says, our mind has Velcro for the bad stuff and Teflon for the good stuff.

If we are in a fear-based state, we will limit our possibilities to be open to new perspectives, get new ideas and see new ways of working. Self-compassion practices are a way to actively balance any tendencies to be overly self-critical and find a more relaxed stance toward both us and the situation we are facing.

The Center for Systems Awareness,[11] co-founded by Peter Senge, offers a program on Compassionate Systems Leadership where a wide variety of tools are shared related to navigating in complex situations. As a part of the program, the term leadership is explored and Senge points to that the root meaning of leading refers to 'stepping over a threshold and into the unknown'. In that understanding of leadership lies an implicit acceptance that we will likely make mistakes along the way.

In the context of leading changes in complex systems, Senge and his colleagues also highlights the need for courage and vulnerability. Courage here refers to our willingness to approach a situation with an open mind and open heart. Vulnerability is about being open to help from others.

It can be argued that all the traits above hinges on our ability to be committed, yet self-compassionate. But how can we concretely practice this self-compassion when we find ourselves struggling to find a solution to a difficult problem? Below we revisit Kristin Neff's three pillars of practicing self-compassion, in the context of facing wicked problems.

### Being mindful

In the section about self-awareness, we used the metaphor of riding a bike. To keep our balance on a bike, as well as to keep our mental balance, a key skill is to quickly notice when we are starting to lose our balance.

When we are facing a complex and challenging situation, chances are that we will start to tense up, both physically and mentally. As we have covered already, this is normal and to be expected, but we don't have to get stuck in that state.

The 'being mindful' part of self-compassion is about noticing and accepting your own reactions. A good starting point is paying attention to your physical state. Bring awareness to your body and to notice if you are tensing up somewhere. If so, tune in your attention on where you feel the tension. Without forcing it, see if you can let your awareness soften the physical tension and let it melt away. Relaxing physically has an interesting side effect that it also relaxes our mind. Just as troubling thoughts can make our body contract, deliberately relaxing our muscles also has a soothing effect on our mental state.

In the same manner we can pay attention to our mental processes and what thoughts and narratives are dominating our mind. If we notice harsh and self-critical self-talk, we can remind ourselves that these are just though-patterns and not the truth. Just as we can invite our muscles to soften in tensed areas of the body, we can hold our critical thoughts lightly and see if we can let them soften a bit.

Being mindful of physical tension or difficult thoughts doesn't necessarily make them go away, but it can create some 'space' around them. By noticing and observing them for what they are – emotional and mental patterns – we don't have to hold them as the 'truth', and we can be less ruled by them.

### Connecting to our shared humanity

Another aspect of self-compassion is reflecting on how our feelings of uncertainty and discomfort are a normal reaction to challenging circumstances. All humans experience this to one degree or the other, so there is no reason to deny these feelings or be ashamed of them.

Suppressing these kinds of feelings doesn't make them go away, it rather makes them work under cover. As developmental psychologist Robert Kegan says, 'if we can't admit that we have feelings, our feelings will have us.

Paradoxically, by admitting our feelings of discomfort to ourselves, we get less prone to act unconsciously on them. Getting them out in the open and viewing them as a normal part of navigating in complex environment, we can reflect on how best to respond, apply agency and act wisely.

### Applying kindness

The third aspect to self-compassion is to approach ourselves with the same kind attitude as we would with a friend. To put this into the context of facing a wicked and challenging problem, we would probably be compassionate, supportive, and helpful to our friends, not put pressure on them to 'get it right'.

As we looked at before, being kind is not the same as letting ourselves 'off the hook'. We can still hold on to our aspiration to find a solution or improve a situation, but we apply a kind of *fierce gentleness*, committing ourselves to be both outcome oriented and kind at the same time.

A natural outcome of applying this attitude is that we become more willing to test ideas, learn from mistakes and try again. All traits that are key when working in iterations to solve complex problems.

## Awareness and clear seeing

Especially when stressed, we can easily start operating on autopilot and navigate our world based on our old assumptions rather than sensing what is really happening. The second area we can train to get better at working with complex problems is to cultivate our attention, nurture our curiosity and deepen our awareness.

When facing complexity and uncertainty, we can turn our attention both inwards and outwards, noticing patterns in ourselves as well as around us. We will start looking at how we can explore and understand our own biases and mental models, and by uncovering them, we might be able to see new possibilities and potential solutions to the challenges we face.

### Inward awareness – exploring our mental models

The historian Yuval Noah Harari[12] became world famous through his book *Sapiens – a brief history about humankind,* where he explores why Homo Sapiens of all species came to dominate our planet. One of the core human traits Harari focuses on is our ability to believe in stories. Stories don't have to be true, but as long as we believe in the same story or 'truth', we can collaborate in large numbers.

In his work, Harari shows how stories, or shared mental models, has helped humans build societies, create religions that span across continents, create global trade networks, and more. Mental models can lead to both beneficial and destructive behaviors. Shared beliefs in human rights have made people and nations work together to improve living conditions. Beliefs around certain nations' supremacy have led to wars and atrocities. People having competing mental models and not being willing to understand and relate to each other's beliefs have throughout history been the seed of conflict.

One of the core messages in *Sapiens* is that we should be careful to take our own mental models for being the truth. History has shown us that what we believe to be true and right today, will be seen in a different light in the future. This is why we might want to hold our current mental models lightly when we are facing a new situation, or when leading our organisation through a complex transformation.

### The necessity and limitations of mental models

Mental models can be understood as a set of beliefs and assumptions that help our mind to make sense of reality. The benefits are, for example, that we can save time and energy by relating something we see to an existing mental model, and quickly know how to respond to the situation. Mental models help us leverage our knowledge and experiences, and having shared mental models helps us collaborate more efficiently together with others.

However, our mental models can also create limitations to what we can see, hear, and think. The term *confirmation bias* refers to our brain's tendency to pay attention to what fits with our current mental model and filter out data that points in other directions. When we find ourselves facing a situation that requires new approaches, we must learn to explore and hold our mental models lightly.

### Another level of self-awareness and mindfulness practice

Self-awareness and mindfulness run as a theme through this book, and we have earlier explored different aspects, like becoming aware of where our attention is in this very moment, or noticing thoughts and emotions as they arise. We have also looked at self-awareness through the lens of personality profiles, for example, whether we have a natural preference for focusing on details or like visionary thinking.

In the following sections, we will explore the next level of self-awareness as we look at our mental models and the assumptions and beliefs that underpin them. What we explore here relates back to the self-awareness practices we worked with earlier, we just expand the scope.

One of the practices we can refer back to here is mindfulness meditation. In the previous mindfulness practices, we mainly directed our awareness toward sensations, thoughts and emotions happening in the current moment. With the same basic approach, we can start noticing patterns that repeat themselves over time when we do our practice.

By paying attention to the thoughts and narratives that show up in our mind, in formal meditation practice or otherwise, we can notice that there are reoccurring themes. This can be certain emotions that frequently show up, thoughts about us or other people that keep popping up or ruminations about things we worry about. When we practice noticing these patterns, it is important to apply a non-judgmental attitude toward ourselves. There is no use in classifying our mental patterns as 'good' or 'bad', but rather stay curious about them.

Over time, the patterns we gravitate back to give us a clue about mental models, beliefs, and assumptions that might be guiding our thinking processes. Starting to notice these patterns opens the door to exploring them further.

### The ladder of inference

When we start to recognise and identify our mental models it can be worth the effort to explore their roots. A helpful tool often used in systems theory is the so-called *ladder of inference*. It is attributed to Chris Argyris, a professor at both Yale and Harvard in the field of organisational development and learning but has been used by many other thought leaders and in many contexts.

The idea of the ladder of inference is to explore how we end up believing what we hold to be true. If we approach the process with curiosity and full honesty, it can be enlightening, at times a bit embarrassing and often very helpful – if we want to break out of a mental model.

The ladder consists of seven steps, showing how we go from observing data to creating our own beliefs and acting based on them.

The process of going from raw data to firmly held beliefs can stretch over a long time, but sometimes be very fast. Especially if what we experience has similarities to other situations for which we already have a well-developed belief. Our mind can take a short cut and 'borrow' assumptions and conclusions from similar experiences.

Our brain needs to save time and energy by reusing assumptions and mental models. In many scenarios this can be helpful, but when facing complex situations or important decisions, we must be aware of the risks. This energy saving function of the brain can lead us to forming misguided

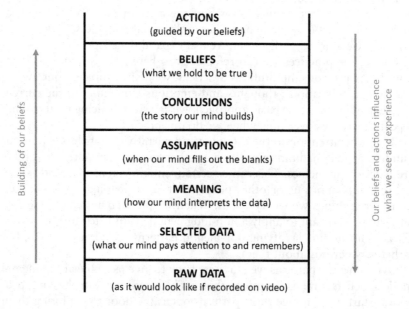

*Figure 3.3* The ladder of inference.

beliefs and mental models that limit our perspectives. This mental process also lies at the core of how our actions subconsciously can become guided by biases.

### Applying the ladder of inference

Using the ladder of inference doesn't have to be driven by a specific problem or conflict. It can be a helpful tool to just practice curiosity and in a gentle way challenge our mental models.

Imagine that you have noticed a certain belief about yourself or others that show up again and again. Using the ladder of inference can help you see how this belief influences your actions and maybe even how you take in information and interpret the world. You can also use the ladder to track your belief back to its root. In this process, it is important to maintain both self-honesty and self-compassion. It is counterproductive to beat ourselves up, we just want to learn and become wiser.

When working on a complex problem, our beliefs and mental models can potentially be a barrier for the creative process. You can try writing down the assumptions and beliefs you have related to the situation, and then explore the ladder of inference on all these beliefs. Test whether they seem to hold up to the scrutiny of your observation, or if your beliefs need to be updated.

If you are working together with others around a complex issue, there are likely to be many different mental models at play. By using the ladder for inference as a framework, you can invite everyone to verbalise their beliefs and what they are founded on. You can even let everyone visualise their ladders and invite a curious reflection on how and why you might see and interpret things differently.

Working with the ladder for inference is not about making anything or anyone right or wrong. It is all about creating awareness about our mental models, so we can understand ourselves and each other better. With this level of awareness, we can choose to challenge our beliefs if necessary, and move beyond any limitations our mental models have set for us.

### Direct perception – training to get to the bottom of the ladder

Our mind is a sensemaking machine, interpreting sense perceptions and putting pieces of information into concepts and stories we can relate to. If we want to train our ability to observe raw data without getting caught up in preconceptions, there is a simple practice we can do called *direct perception*. Below it is described as you would do it as a part of a formal mindfulness practice, but you can also apply the same principles in an everyday situation.

- *Take a comfortable seat and close your eyes*
- *Take of few deep breaths to settle in and allow your body to relax*
- *For a moment, place your attention on your breath and just observe the flow of air in and out*
- *Now shift the attention to sounds around you – what do you hear?*
- *Place your attention on the sound itself – what is the character of the sound?*
- *Notice when your mind starts to create stories and pictures related to the sound*
- *See if you can direct your attention back to the raw sensation of the sound itself, without any interpretations attached to it*
- *What our brains interpret as a sound is originally just air waves hitting your ear drum – what does it feel like for your ear before your mind creates the story?*
- *Notice what other sounds are present and repeat the same curious exploration with other sounds*
- *Now, slowly open your eyes and let you gaze rest on what is in front of you*
- *Your mind will start interpreting the data that comes from your optic nerve into objects, but see if you can notice the raw visual data – light, colours, contours...*
- *Notice how what you observe triggers different kinds of thoughts in you*
- *When you notice that your mind goes into a train of thoughts, see if you can bring your attention back to the raw visual data hitting your retina*
- *To finish the practice, return you attention to the breath and let it rest for a moment before your carry on with your day*

The direct perception practice can seem a bit weird at first as we are so used to relate to our conceptual understandings of what a sound is or what a visual impression means. Training ourselves to peel away our interpretations and focus on the raw data is good for our 'attention muscle', but it also makes us more aware about how quickly our mind always wants to climb up the ladder of inference.

### Exploring our immunities to change

Another way to explore our mental models is the using the Immunity to Change[13] framework, developed by Lisa Lahey and Robert Kegan, both at Harvard University. Where many change models focus on rational analysis and planning, Immunity to Change looks at underlying and often subconscious assumptions that can keep us from developing ourselves or succeeding with transforming our organisations.

Lahey and Kegan have spent decades studying what the psychological mechanisms are that keep smart and rational people stuck in old behaviors, even when they have decided to change. Kegan and Lahey argue that when facing familiar or so-called technical challenges, we can apply rational analyses, planning and discipline to succeed. But, when facing complex or adaptive challenges, i.e. situations that require us to more fundamentally change our way of thinking and working, we need to go deeper down in our psyche. We need to uncover the underlying assumptions and beliefs that risk keeping us stuck in old behaviors.

Immunities To Change is too deep a concept to be appropriately explained here, and my aspiration is therefore only to introduce the key principles to spark your interest. If you sense this could be helpful, I highly recommend you explore more about Lahey and Kegan's work.

### What assumptions keep you from succeeding with change?

If a change is technical and straight forward, you can probably succeed with it by taking your time to set clear goals and make a detailed enough project or action plan. But if you have tried that and still fail in changing the necessary behaviors, you probably have to do what Lahey and Kegan call an 'immunity map'.

Instead of beating ourselves for not following through on our change plans, Immunities To Change mapping offers a more compassionate approach by trying to understand the underlying reasons for why we might be stuck in old ways of working. Lahey and Kegan call this looking for 'competing commitments'. A competing commitment can be something we subconsciously care about, and which pulls us in a different direction compared to our conscious and rational commitments.

At the core of the immunity mapping process lies uncovering the different things we are committed to in life. These can be commitments related to our work and career, but also to our family, our values, or the community we are a part of. Often some of these commitments can be competing with each other, which can get us stuck.

When we find ourselves stuck in a situation with competing commitments and no apparent solution for how to move forward, it can help to take a deeper look at our commitments and what underpins them. This is where we come back to assumptions, beliefs, and mental models.

Kegan and Lahey argue that to get unstuck and work through an 'immunity to change', we must understand what underlying assumptions and beliefs function as drivers for our different commitments. Just as when working with the ladder of inference, this process requires some courage and a lot of honesty. On closer examination, the beliefs we uncover can surprise and even embarrass us. They are not always rational but built on fragmented data and assumptions. Again, it is important to bring a good portion of self-compassion into this. Whatever assumptions and beliefs we discover, are there for a good reason. Our previous experiences in life have led us to these, and these mental models have probably served us one way or the other along the way.

If we work seriously with mapping our immune system and try to deeply understand our underlying beliefs and mental models, the process will take us to a point of choice, where we can decide to hold our beliefs as being true for us and keep operating from them, or choose to challenge them. If we find that our assumptions and beliefs could use an upgrade, below are a few questions we can use for reflection.

- *Where do these beliefs stem from?*
  - Here you can use the ladder of inference again
- *Has anything changed since you experienced the things that led to this belief?*
- *How is this belief influencing your behavior, actions, and priorities today?*
- *What would be possible if this belief would prove not to be 100% true?*
- *What can be a safe way for you to test if the assumptions underpinning this belief are still correct?*
- *Are there other ways you can experiment and collect data to update your belief?*

To paraphrase Robert Kegan again, 'if we are not aware about the assumptions we have, our assumptions will have us'. Our beliefs and mental models guide our lives. They can help us but also create mental prisons that limit our personal growth and the potential to succeed with necessary transformations on a personal level, in our organisations or in society.

### Outward awareness – understanding the context around us

The same way we can explore our inner world, we can also approach the world around us with curiosity and an aspiration to understand underlying patterns. Especially when addressing difficult and complex challenges, it is easy to get caught up in solving the problem symptoms, without really understanding the conditions that might be causing them. To get to the root of an issue requires working with a more systemic approach, i.e. to try to understand the underlying patterns and interacting structures that produce the results we can observe.

## Mapping the systems iceberg

A great source of inspiration when it comes to systemic thinking and leadership is Peter Senge,[14] a senior lecturer at MIT, and author of best-selling books such as *Presence* and *The Fifth Discipline*. When trying to better understand a complex situation we are facing, a useful model often used by Peter Senge is the so-called systems iceberg. The iceberg model helps us explore the multiple layers to a situation where only the ones close to the surface are easily visible.

To use an example for how to apply the systems iceberg model, let us look at a strategy implementation effort struggling to move forward. The top of the iceberg would represent independent *events we can observe*. In the case of a strategy implementation effort, this could, for example, be that we notice that a certain department is slowing down the implementation process by not prioritising resources to an agreed project.

When we apply a systemic view to a situation, we look both at individual events, but more importantly we look for patterns. Just below the surface is the next level in the iceberg model, the less obvious but important *reoccurring patterns*. In the case of a failing strategy implementation, we might notice that there are multiple departments that one way or the other come up short when it comes to prioritising time and resources to new and strategically important initiatives.

When we have started to identify patterns, we go one step deeper, looking for *underlying structures* that might produce these patterns. These structures can be, for examples, assumptions and mental models that

*Figure 3.4* The Systems Iceberg.

govern our thinking. It can also be organisational structures that lead to certain behaviors, or physical structures that influence how we work.

Using our strategy implementation case, an example of a mental structure can be that people in the organisation have previous bad experiences with implementing new strategic initiatives and therefore carry assumptions that 'this effort won't work either'. With these conscious or subconscious assumptions, people are likely to be reluctant to put too much effort into this new strategy. An example of an organisational structure that acts as a barrier to a strategy implementation could be an incentive system that rewards people for keeping doing what they have done previously.

These are just some examples of what can emerge when we start to pay attention and be curious about the reoccurring patterns and underlying structures in a situation and explore how different elements may influence and interact with each other. Uncovering these things can give us a better understanding and more perspectives on how we can work to improve a situation.

Applying and experimenting with the systems iceberg model is a helpful way to widen and deepen our understanding of a situation and is also a useful tool to involve others in thinking together around a complex challenge. It often helps to work visually on a whiteboard, flipchart, a digital Miro Board or similar.

### The way we listen determine what we can notice

When we interact with the world around us, the way we listen will influence the relationships we can build, and what information we will take in. Listening in this sense is more than just being quiet. It is equally about our attitude and level of openness to other perspectives.

Cultivating our listening skills takes practice and a lot of self-awareness and is an important part of developing our capacity for really understanding complex situations. One of the most useful approaches for understanding levels of listening that I have come across is from Otto Scharmer,[15] a senior lecturer at MIT, author of Theory U and founder of the Presencing Institute.

Scharmer has dedicated his career to understanding the dynamics of transformations in individuals, organisations, and societies, and how we can address the complex challenges of our time. Based on his research and experiences with this topic over many decades, he holds listening, in its wider sense, as maybe the most important leadership capability.

Scharmer often describes four levels of listening,[16] each offering a different quality of openness to the situation at hand or the people we are interacting with. Inspired by Scharmer's work, I often use the descriptions below as ways to understand and explore how to listen well.

*Listening at level 1 — confirming the things we already know*

If we don't work actively with how we listen, we will often come to operate from level 1. This means that we listen from the center of our own assumptions and interpret what we see and hear through the filters of what we already know. At this level of listening, we will tend to mostly notice things that fit with what we already know and think.

An example of this from my own experience comes from watching a political debate on TV together with my wife a few years ago. After the broadcast was over and we had turned off the TV, we discussed what had been said, and interestingly enough, we recalled different facts from the interview. As we have slightly different political views, I had noticed and remembered facts and arguments that fit my views, while my wife had noted other pieces of data that strengthened her position.

Being in the confirming mode is often the default mode for our mind for the simple reason that it saves our brain a lot of time and energy. As we have covered in earlier chapters, the subconscious parts of our brain constantly compare inputs from the world around us with our previous experiences and mental models, and quickly draw conclusions based on that.

This is in many ways a very effective and comfortable way to navigate the world, but we also run the risk of what in psychology is called *confirmation bias*. When our brain orients toward information that confirms what we already think, we can get cemented in our views and miss out on important new data we need to navigate life skilfully. This confirmation bias is a natural inclination of our human mind, but on top of that, internet and social media algorithms accelerate this tendency today, with the risk of placing us in an 'echo chamber' where we only take in information that confirms our current point of view.

The bottom line here is that we must acknowledge that the confirming mindset of level 1 listening is a natural default mode of our mind. To start to listen with an open mind, we must make an effort to move to level 2.

*Listening at level 2 — curiously looking for new facts*

Every time we become aware of our biases or 'confirming' mindset, we can consciously shift to listening with more openness and curiosity. This is where we actively search for information that is new and maybe even disturbing to us.

It is said that Charles Darwin carried around a notebook where he wrote down things he had observed that <u>disconfirmed</u> his theories. As a good scientist, he was keen to collect all data, both the things that fit with what he thought and the things that challenged it. That way, he could over time expand his understanding of a field of interest.

When we start listening with curiosity, we metaphorically move out from the center of our assumptions and start 'looking out through the window' to observe what else is out there to be discovered.

To apply this approach in daily life, we can practice asking open and curious questions. When we feel the urge to interrupt or argue back in a discussion, we can practice pausing and keep listening with as open a mind as possible. And even as we listen, we can notice the difference between when our mind is silently having judgments and opinions about what is being said, and when we can really take in what other people are saying with true openness.

Just to be clear, there are, of course, many situations where we need to disagree and argue for our own point view. Practicing level 2 listening is not about holding back our own knowledge and opinions, but about making sure we are open to all data and information, so we can understand different aspects of a situation as thoroughly as possible.

### Listening at level 3 – approaching with empathy

The first step toward deep listening is to be open to facts and information, but there is more to true listening than gathering objective data. The next level is to start relating to an issue from the other party's perspective. This means stepping out of our own position and beliefs and then turning the perspectives around to try to understand how things are experienced by other people involved.

Empathic listening includes both the cognitive process of understanding another person's point of view, but also so-called emotional resonance. The latter is the ability to relate to and sense what another person is feeling and what their needs are.

Let us take an example when we are in a disagreement or a conflict. Level 2 listening would be to be open to facts that we previously might have been blind to. Level 3 would be to go beyond the facts and try to relate to what feelings and emotions the other person is experiencing. By applying empathic listening, we are connecting to the humanity of other people involved and collect what we can call emotional data. How people feel around a situation can be as important as objective data, to know how to navigate a complex situation.

### Listening at level 4 – opening for what wants to emerge

This level of listening is not really something we can just turn on. It is rather a phenomenon that can emerge when two or more people are applying level 2 and 3 listening together. When everyone is willing to 'step out' of their conditioned way of thinking and be truly open to each other and the possibilities of new perspectives, listening can become a generative process. This is where new ideas can emerge that no one could have thought of individually.

We could also call this co-creative listening. No one needs to be right or win a discussion. Instead, the group's focus and energy are channelled toward building on each other's perspectives without prestige, to be able explore new territory together.

Hopefully, you have experienced this sense of openness, creativity, and flow between people, maybe at work or in other contexts.

### Paying attention to our level of listening

Listening well may sound like common sense, but as said before: common sense is not always common practice. In the context of addressing complex situations in our life, the level of openness and curiosity we can bring into conversations will have a great influence on what patterns we can detect, what possibilities we can see and how skilfully we can co-create solutions with others.

A core practice all of us can work on is to regularly pause to notice our attitude toward a situation and at what level we are currently listening. It is important not to beat ourselves up when we realise we may not listen as deeply and openly as we would like to do. The point here is to create more awareness, so we can adjust our approach and cultivate our ability to be curious, empathic and open to all perspectives and possibilities.

For the purpose of this chapter, we will not go deeper into tools, techniques and theories related to listening or mapping systems. The key message we can bring with us from the field of systems thinking however, is that working with complex situations requires cultivating curiosity and paying close attention. This helps us create greater awareness and understanding of both ourselves and the surrounding context we navigate in.

To learn more about how to work with complex systems, I can recommend the Center for Systems Awareness[17] who offers inspiration, free resources as well as training programs. Another great resource is Presencing Institute[18] who also offers a wide range of free classes and courses, as well programs for those who want to go deeper.

## Skillful use of intentions and aspirations

When facing a complex challenge or navigating in the uncertainty of a transformation process, it can often be difficult to define clear, measurable goals and make very specific plans. As a matter of fact, trying to do just that can be counterproductive as it may make us too stuck with our plan and less responsive to what emerges along the way.

But not having a set goal and a defined action plan isn't the same thing as not having a sense of direction. As we touched on in a previous section on Awareness Based Change, having clear intention can be a crucial element when navigating in change. We might not be sure about exactly what road to take, but we know in what direction we are heading.

A clear sense of direction guides attention and awareness toward a desired outcome and supports the creative process. This sense of direction can take the form of a personal aspiration, a vision for an organisation, etc. The trick here is to find the relevant balance between having enough of a clear vision to guide and inspire, and yet not becoming too attached to a specific outcome.

History shows us visionary people who have faced difficult and complex situations and changed the world by being able to see possibilities other people could not yet see. This can be the work of Mahatma Gandhi who was able to guide India to independence through the principles of non-violent non-cooperation, or Steve Jobs who enabled Apple to create new types of products using existing technology.

Their success and innovations didn't come out of a carefully tailored masterplan based on analyses, but rather through years and decades of exploring the boundaries of the unknown and trying their way forward. What led them forward was probably not a detailed and fixed roadmap, but rather a vision that gave them guidance. Using envisioning can be a helpful tool when working our own way through unknown territory.

### Using envisioning to prime our brain and guide our mind

You may worry that envisioning is a bit new age and that we place our hope to some kind of metaphysical support. Although some people and traditions may have faith in these kinds of ideas, there are actually neurological reasons for why envisioning a desired outcome can be helpful when working in complex situations.

Our brain is constantly exposed to many more sense impressions and much more data than it can process, it will therefore naturally filter away most of the inputs and focus on what it believes to be most relevant and important (also see the section on Ladder of Inference). By envisioning something, we prime our brain to start paying attention to data related to and supportive of that vision. When we do that, information starts to 'appear' that relates to our vision. The data was, of course, there all the time, but by activating our subconscious mental 'radar', we start noticing it.

An example of this feature of our mind is when we are thinking about buying a new car and might have become interested in a specific brand, let's say a Volvo. Suddenly, we start noticing Volvo cars more frequently. Or when we or someone close to us are pregnant, we notice baby strollers everywhere. When working with complex problems we can leverage this feature of our mind. By priming our mind, the subconscious regions of our brain can work for us and pick up on subtle pieces of data or see the patterns in what appears to be random information.

To activate and use this potential we can use a wide variation of envisioning practices. Below is an example that can be used for setting a direction in your own life. You can, of course, tweak it to fit the context that is relevant for you.

### Envisioning a desired future

This practice combines mental visualisation with journaling or flow-writing, so please have pen and paper or another preferred note-taking device ready.

 Start with a few minutes of flow-writing, based on the questions below. Take a minute or two on each of the questions. You don't have to analyse too much; rather let your pen flow and see what comes down when you contemplate the questions.

- *What is truly important to you in life?*
- *What are some of the values that you hold most dearly?*
- *What do you want to accomplish?*
- *How would accomplishing that have an impact on you, people around you and your environment?*

When you have finished your writing, put your pen and paper aside for a moment. Close your eyes and settle into a comfortable position. Take a few deep breaths where you deliberately let your body relax.

We are now going to visualise what a possible future could look like if things turned out in the most favourable way. You can use a time horizon that suits the purpose of your envisioning, may it be a situation a month away, a goal for the end of the year, or more profound changes requiring a couple of years to materialise.

Let us start with your personal experience, health, and well-being:

- *Picture yourself in the future imagining that things turn out in the most favourable way.*
- *Where are you?*
- *What do you see around you?*

- *How are you feeling in this future scenario?*
- *How is your energy?*
- *What feels especially meaningful for you?*

Now let us explore the realm of your relationships, family, friends, and colleagues:

- *Picturing yourself in a perfect future scenario, what do your relations look like?*
- *How are you enjoying relationships with others?*
- *In what ways are your closest relationships important to you?*
- *How do you contribute to and invest in the strengthening of these relationships?*

Finally, visualise the realm of work or other ways you influence the world around you:

- *Picturing a perfect future, what do you spend most of your time with?*
- *Where are you, and what do you see around you?*
- *What feels deeply meaningful for you?*
- *How do you contribute to others and what do others appreciate about you?*
- *Stay with the visualisations in your mind for a minute more while you are noticing the flow of your own breathing. Stay with whatever sensations, emotions or feelings that are present.*
- *When you feel ready, you can open your eyes and come back. If you feel like adding more things to your writing you can do so, otherwise you can wrap up your practice.*

In our brain, there is little difference between how neurons fire together when we visualise something, compared to experiencing the same event in real life. The visualisation practice is therefore a way for us to familiarise our brain with scenarios we would like to see more of and orient its activity toward those possibilities.

You can experiment with using envision both related to personal and professional situations and see how it helps you create a clearer picture of your intentions and aspirations.

### The Stockdale paradox

There is, of course, a fine line between cultivating a positive vision and becoming disconnected from reality. The story of Admiral Jim Stockdale, an US pilot being shot down over North Vietnam during the wars and held in a POW camp for over 7 years, illustrates the paradoxical ability of having faith in a good outcome and at the same time being able to face the hard facts of reality.

When Stockdale was interviewed by Jim Collins for the book *From Good to Great*,[19] Collins asked him what made him survive, where so many of his co-prisoners perished. The essence of Stockdale's experience what that those who lacked faith that they would ever get out of the prison camp, didn't have the inner motivation to live through the hardships. However, the optimists who kept saying to themselves that they would be home soon, died of broken hearts when their hopes didn't materialise. What Stockdale did was to hold the paradox. He kept the vision of being reunited with his family alive in himself, and at the same time faced the reality that it would most likely take a long time and be a very difficult period.

> *You must never confuse faith that you will prevail in the end—which you can never afford to lose—with the discipline to confront the most brutal facts of your current reality, whatever they might be.*
> Admiral Jim Stockdale

This ability to hold the paradox of seeing current reality clearly (what we in previous sections talked about as awareness) and at the same time holding a motivating aspiration helped Stockdale through years of hardship and uncertainty. The so-called Stockdale paradox can probably be a helpful principle for all of us when facing challenging situations.

### Holding the creative tension

Another way of describing what Stockdale pointed to is the term *creative tension* we have touched on earlier. Most of the time, there will be a gap between our desired state and current reality. This gap creates a psychological tension that we can experience as frustration, disappointment, etc. But this tension can also be a source of energy and creativity. Without that tension we might not be motivated to act.

If we don't have the capacity to hold the creative tension in ourselves or our organisation, we will want to reduce the tension by doing one of two things; lower our aspirations or imagine our current reality better than it is.

To navigate skilfully in change, transformation, and complexity, we must learn to accept and befriend the creative tension. Our so-called *negative capability* that we addressed earlier, helps us stay with the discomfort and frustrations without becoming reactive, projecting blame on others, etc. Instead, we can use the energy for creativity and constructive action.

*Having a clear direction, but holding our plans lightly*

Let us wrap up this part by reminding ourselves that a core characteristic of complex challenges is that they typically contain a multitude of interrelated elements that influence each other in unpredictable ways. Therefore, we cannot expect to get from A to B according to a predetermined plan. Navigating in this context is rather about skilfully using a combination of three elements:

- Having an aspiration and intention that gives us a sense of direction
- Paying attention and becoming aware of patterns and underlying structures
- Being responsive and flexible to what emerges

In our next part, we are going to explore our mind's subconscious capacity for pattern recognition and creativity, and how we can leverage that when we are addressing complex situations.

## Working with intuition and emergence

We live in a society that praises analysis and rationale, and for good reasons. Thanks to these traits, we have developed many helpful systems, structures, and technologies. As we touched on earlier, our cognitive capacities for logical and rational thinking play an important role in planning, structuring, and solving complicated problems.

However, when it comes to complex problems, our analyses and rationale may not be enough. We may need to explore other capacities in the human brain, what we could call more intuitive intelligence. As we touched on in earlier sections, this is what professor Dan Siegel at UCLA refers to when he talks about integrating both the left- and right-brain modes.

Now, intuition or 'gut-feeling' can sometimes be written off as wuh-wuh, but there are some straight forward scientific explanations to these abilities. In this section we will unpack how some of the subconscious regions of the brain work, and what we can do to access these abilities when needed.

### The role of feelings and intuition when navigating in unknown territory

In an experiment known as the University of Iowa Gambling Task,[20] Bechara and his colleagues, had participants perform a simulated gambling task, where they could win or lose money based on what cards they drew. Participants were placed in front of four decks of cards, which were secretly prepared so two of the decks contained 'good' cards that would make participants win money, and two of them contained 'bad' cards that would make them lose money.

The cards were arranged so the pattern of good/bad decks would not show immediately but would emerge after a while as participants tested their way forward by pulling cards from the different decks. The parallel here is, of course, complex problem solving, where we can only find the pattern that holds the key to the solution, by testing our way forward.

Participants in the study were told they would be drawing a total of 100 cards and given instructions to let the research leaders know if and when they could start detecting any patterns in the cards. They were also being hooked up to a machine that measured their skin conductance response, a commonly used indicator for stress or anxiety.

The results from the study showed that participants on average needed 80 cards to conclude which two decks were the 'good ones' that made them win money, and which decks they should stay away from. But already after 50 cards, most of participants had started to express a hunch about which were the 'bad' decks. The most interesting part of the study, however, was that after only ten cards, the participants' bodies started showing stress reactions (sweating hands) every time they reached for a card from one of the 'bad' decks. Apparently, something in their brain had already detected the pattern, and tried to send a warning signal to have them avoid the 'bad decks'.

Neuroscientists credit this pattern detection ability to parts of our limbic system that through evolution has developed the ability to quickly process data and warn us if there is something we need to react to. As this process happens in the more subconscious levels of our brain, our rational neo cortex will not pick up on these warning signals immediately.

However, from the limbic system there is a well-developed network of neural connection leading out to the heart and gut region, and then on out into our bodies. Any reaction in our limbic system can therefore, for biological reasons, be noticed in our bodies, before the upper, analytical, and rational parts of our brain have picked up, processed, and understood the signal. This is the neurological explanation of what we normally know as a 'gut-feeling'.

When our subconscious limbic system has detected a pattern in the endless stream of data and information we meet every day, and tries to inform us about it, we will notice it as subtle sensation at first, long before we cognitively can start to understand the message.

### The computing power of our limbic system

There has been done quite a lot of research trying to specify the differences in computing power between the limbic system and the more rational neo cortex. Even if different studies end up with different numbers on it, the message is clear; the lower, subconscious systems of our brain can take in and process much larger amounts of data than the more newly developed parts of our brain. Although the human neo cortex is very good at rational analyses and precision, it has a limited processing capacity and is rather slow. If we can learn to leverage the amazing processing power of our earlier developed limbic system, it can help us when navigating in complex environments or when we must make decisions based on limited and scattered data.

In his book *Blink*,[21] author Malcolm Gladwell describes our brain's ability to read patterns and draw conclusions based on limited information. He calls the phenomenon *'thin-slicing'*. With only a thin slice of information, our brain can make sense of a situation, draw conclusions and act on it. An example described is a research study where lay people got to watch married couples through a glass mirror. Based on their impressions of how the couples were interacting, they were asked to predict if their marriage would hold long-term or not. Despite the short impressions they got of the couples, people's predictions turned out to be surprisingly accurate.

Gladwell also describes how 'thin-slicing' is an important feature of the brain, for example, for fire fighters or police who must take in-the-moment decisions with little data or time for analyses. These professionals have stored a lot of accumulated experiences through their work and training. When facing a complex situation, their limbic system can take in the available data, process it quickly to see patterns, reference it with their internal database of experiences and then get a hunch for how to act.

The bottom line from the Iowa Gambling Task, the studies Gladwell refers to as well as much other research, is, that what we in daily language call intuition is a real and useful feature of our brain. It is not mystical, but an important function we have developed through evolution to survive and thrive.

In the context of working with complex challenges where it is difficult to think and analyse our way toward the right answers, we can potentially leverage this function and allow the pattern recognition and computing capacity of the limbic system to help us. Later in this section, we will explore concrete methods for doing that, but before that, a note of caution.

### The dark side of intuition – beware of biases

As mentioned, a part of the process leading to a 'hunch' is that our brain compares the data at hand to previous experiences stored in our mental database. That way, we can leverage what we have learned and use that to quickly come to a conclusion. But what if our database is outdated? What if the situation we have in front of us is profoundly different from what we have experienced before?

In Blink, Malcolm Gladwell brings up the example of the police shooting unarmed and innocent black people. The police officers' limbic systems probably interpreted a situation based on a combination of previous experiences and biases, which let them to react in a disastrous way. Few of us must face as difficult and potentially fatal decision-making situations as police officers, but we can all fall into the trap of misinterpreting a situation and make the wrong calls based on our biases.

Working with intuition therefore comes with a warning sign – Beware of Biases! It requires us to check our assumptions, be aware and curious about what previous experiences may trigger our gut-feelings and question whether that old data is a relevant reference point for the situation we are currently facing. The Ladder of Inference we explored earlier can be a helpful tool here.

To connect to another of our earlier sections, we can remember to see emotions as data from the limbic system. But data is not the same as the truth. The message here is that we can and should <u>listen</u> to emotional impulses and 'gut-feelings'. They give us an indication that our limbic system has detected a pattern and wants us to know about. But it is not the same thing as we should always <u>act</u> based on our impulses. We can honor and be curious about the 'data' coming from our limbic system, but we should also engage the rational and analytical capacity of our neo cortex to discern what impulses to believe and act on.

### Combining intuition and rationale

When Swedish Television interviewed Nobel Prize laureates across different fields of research on what role intuition had played in their research, they all told more or less the same story. Their breakthroughs had started with a gut-feeling, an intuitive sense that there was something new to be discovered. But their discoveries only materialised into something useful by applying scientific and rigorous processes and an analytical approach. Their ability to combine their intuitive and their analytical mind helped them toward their Nobel Prizes. With training, we can all get better at leveraging the intuitive intelligence of our limbic system and then use the rational capacity of our neo cortex to quality-check it.

But how do we know if our intuitions are helpful or guided by biases and leading us in the wrong direction? Hopefully some of the approaches and tools we have covered in earlier chapters can help us. We can use our mindfulness practices to watch our emotions and impulses more objectively and become aware of the narratives we have created in our minds. We can use the Ladder of Inference to backtrack our assumptions and check the data behind our intuitions. We can explore our Immunities To Change when we feel drawn into behaviors that are not aligned with our rational goals.

It is also worth noting that much of the activity and signals from our limbic system are for evolutionary reasons driven by fear and self-protection. Even if our fear-based reactions are important and helpful in certain situations, as a rule of thumb it is likely that a disproportional part of them is off the mark, and that we should always 'check the data' when we feel driven by fear.

### Balancing biases by expanding our inner reference points

A way of avoiding being too stuck in our own assumptions and biases is to consciously work to get out of our own 'echo chamber' where the information we are exposed to tends to confirm what we already think and know.

When I was working as a marketing manager, I attended a seminar with an advertising wizard from Texas named Roy Williams. Williams provoked me and all the other marketing professionals in the room by arguing that we all by default were incompetent in perceiving our clients' reality objectively. His point was that we were so entangled in our own knowledge, that we could not see things from an outside perspective. Then Williams delivered this one-liner:

*When you are inside a bottle, it is difficult to read the label*

I have been carrying this simple but profound point with me ever since and use it as a reminder every time I find myself stuck (again) in my own beliefs about what is true.

Exploring and acknowledging our beliefs and mental models are helpful first steps to not being imprisoned by them, but to really go beyond them, we need to work consciously and diligently to expand our reference points. Below are some examples for how to do that.

### Exposing ourselves to new data and different perspectives

Most of us gather our information and input from a limited number of sources. We tend to keep subscribing to the same newspaper and magazines, using the same news feeds, and listening to the same podcasts year after year. No matter how high a quality these sources have, they are still likely to represent a certain view or political standpoint. The information we get through these channels has consciously or subconsciously been filtered before it reaches us.

The people we hang out with in the form of colleagues, neighbors, and friends, are also likely to carry a lot of similarities. You might think that they are a diverse group with many different opinions, but when looking deeper, it is likely that you share a lot of deeper values and beliefs.

There is, of course, nothing wrong with finding a 'tribe' where we feel comfortable or select media channels we like. However, it can bring us into that kind of 'echo chamber' where our beliefs are constantly confirmed by people with the same beliefs. It can be helpful to every now and then expose us to people, views and news that represent different perspectives. You could, for example:

- Make it a habit to regularly read the news on a website you know represent a different political point of view than your own
- Attend events with people who represent different walks of life than your own
- Engage yourself in community work outside your own community
- Subscribe to a podcast on a topic that falls outside your comfort zone

When we expose ourselves to wider sources of inputs, we provide our brain with more data to work with and we increase the chances that our creative mind can make connections and detect new possibilities, not limited to what we previously 'knew'.

There are endless possibilities here. The point is on a regular basis to expose ourselves to new perspectives, and stay open and curios. It is not necessarily easy, and you might not agree with everyone and everything you see. Just see it as a mental workout, expanding your reference points.

### What possibilities can emerge when we don't need to know?

A Japanese zen master, Suzuki Roshi, famously said:

*In the beginner's mind there are many possibilities, in the expert's mind there are few.*

He points to how we, if we don't work with expanding our awareness, can get so occupied with all our existing knowledge and the mental models we have accumulated and created throughout our life, we cannot see potential new perspectives and emerging possibilities.

Another metaphor from the zen tradition is the idea of 'emptying the cup'. If our mental 'cup' is already full of opinions and 'truths' about how things are, it is difficult to take in new ideas. To open ourselves to creativity, we need to empty our cup, i.e. create enough mental space for new things to emerge.

Emergence is an interesting phenomenon, often described as a process where separate entities start to interact with each other, and in that process something new and often unpredicted is created that none of the entities could have produced on their own. This phenomenon is, of course, central in creative processes, hence also in navigating complex situations where we must figure out solutions as we go along.

For emergence to happen, we need to 'empty the cup' and create space for things to happen, by, for example, slowing down or loosening the grip of our own assumptions. This may sound counterintuitive, but vulnerability is in a way a doorway into creativity. When we don't feel the need to be right or to defend ourselves or our point of view, we have greater freedom of action.

We will dive more into the practical aspects of creating mental space in the coming sections. But apart from creating space, we also need to pay attention to our attitude.

### Striving not to strive

Most of us are likely to have had experiences with aha-moments, new insights and ideas suddenly showing up in our mind, not when we were sitting in front of our computer, trying really hard, but when taking a shower, meditating, going for a run, etc.

Facilitating emergence and making it work for us is a paradoxical process. We must work diligently to collect data, set clear intentions, etc., and at the same time we must learn to let go of our need to get quick results. When we try too hard, we tense up and the parts of our brain that support big picture thinking and creative processes get shut down.

As you might remember from one of our previous chapters, our brain moves toward short-term orientation and repetitive patterns when the stress related sympathetic nervous system is activated. When we feel safe and relaxed, we normally have greater access to creativity and bigger perspectives.

The practices we explored in the first sections of the book around 'resetting to calm' can therefore come in handy here. Based on how our brain works, it is much more likely that we can see new solutions to the challenges we are facing, if our nervous system is in a calm state.

### Setting a direction and relaxing into it

Being a performance-oriented person by nature, I do not find it easy to integrate being both outcome oriented and yet relaxed and open to what emerges. My experience is, however, that when I manage to be in this paradox, I get into a better flow and can be more creative and productive, without getting exhausted.

I have learned over time to notice when I am trying too hard and start to tense up. Interestingly, I can notice it first by the physiological signals (see the section on *noticing physiological sensations* in Chapter 2). For me, the early warning is when I can sense my belly, chest and shoulders starting to contract. When I notice these tell-tale signs, I practice turning off the 'struggle switch', take a few deep breaths, consciously allowing my muscles to relax, and asking myself what it would feel like to approach the same task with more ease and relaxation.

To summarise and connect to what we have explored before, we can facilitate the emergence of new ideas by:

- Having a clear sense of what we would like to accomplish
- Exposing ourselves to diverse inspiration and different perspectives
- Creating space to let things 'simmer', i.e. allowing the more subconscious regions of our brain to 'marinate' the different inputs and make connections between them

Interestingly enough, both Gandhi and Jobs who we referred to earlier, combined vision with time for reflection. They were known to be very knowledgeable and smart people, and they also had solid contemplative practices. Gandhi was known to go into solitude and retreat when he searched for a way forward in the difficult struggle for independence. Steve Jobs often referred to his meditation practice as one of the tools that helped him see new possibilities.

In the next sections we are going to summarise some of the concrete practices that can help our intuitive intelligence work for us and support the emergence of new perspectives and ideas.

### Practical ways to get intuition and emergence to work for us

To wrap up this chapter, I would like to list a few practical ways to apply what we have covered. I hope you will notice that we are going to revisit many principles and practices we have explored earlier in the book, connect some dots, and point to how these practices can come into play in the context of working with complexity, emergence, and intuition.

#### Checking in and resetting to calm

If our work is intensive and demanding, chances are that we spend a large amount of our days with a low to medium level of stress response being activated in our nervous system. We can be so used to it that we consider it our normal operating mode.

Even if we are accustomed to this, it can still influence our cognitive functioning toward repeating habitual thinking and behaviors, as well as making us more short-sighted than the situation requires. To get out of this autopilot mode, we can apply some of the practices we explored in Chapter 1.

'Checking in' with ourselves is a self-awareness practice which basically means to stop for a short moment to take stock of how we are feeling. We can do this anywhere and anytime, for example, when transitioning between tasks or meetings.

- *Deliberately stop what you are doing for a short moment and turn your attention inwards*
- *Notice your physical and mental state – how are you doing right now? See if you can do this with an attitude of curiosity and self-compassion*
- *Now, take a few deep breaths where you breathe all the way down into your belly, and let your body relax as much as possible every time you breathe out*
- *Notice if anything shifts in your mental or physical state*
- *When you feel ready, proceed with your next activity*

This kind of short check-in can be done in just one minute, and with practice we can start to notice the effects with just one deep breath and a few seconds of mindful attention. Like building any habit, frequently pausing and checking in with ourselves, will create a routine for how to reset our body and mind to calm, and we become able to ground and calm ourselves even within short amounts of time.

When we shift our neural mode from stress to relaxation, we get easier access to the regions of our brain associated with big picture thinking, creativity as well as what we have called intuition. A short pause and a few deep breaths will, of course, not immediately invite a stream of great insights and new ideas, but the point here is to learn the routine of relaxing both our body and mind. By starting to build shorter and longer spaces into our workday where we relax and clear our mind, we increase the likelihood for us to access our intuitive intelligence and sense new possibilities in the situations we are facing.

### Calibrating with our intention

A practice that works well in combination with the check-in, is calibrating with our intentions and aspirations. In our daily grind, we can get so caught up in busyness, that we lose sight of our long-term aspirations and what is truly important.

Calibrating with our intention is a micro-version of the envisioning practice we explored earlier. The basic idea is the same – to remind our brain of what we want to accomplish so we invite both our conscious and subconscious mental processes to support that.

We can do this calibration by just asking ourselves a few questions along these lines:

- *What is my highest aspiration?*
- *What does the situation I have in front of me now, call for?*
- *How can I best contribute?*
- *What is most important right now?*
- *How can I do this in a way that aligns with my long-term aspirations?*

We can find our own questions that work for us. The essence here is to help ourselves get perspectives on the situation we are in, and to calibrate our actions toward what we want to accomplish in the bigger perspective. It can be done before starting any activity or when you feel a bit over-whelmed and need to pause and think through your next steps.

When working with complex problems, we often have to move forward in many small iterations where we can risk losing touch with the bigger picture and end goal. Calibrating with what is the long-term purpose of what we are doing, can help keep us on track. We can liken this with steering a boat through stormy waters at night. We might not know our exact position or be able to see our destination, but by checking the compass on a regular basis, we can at least make sure we are heading in the right direction.

### Applications in meetings and groups

The practices above have been described as individual practices but can, of course, be applied in group settings as well. Depending on the group and how well you know them, these practices can be done with a light touch or as a deeper reflection together.

Below is a form of group check-in that I have used in many different contexts to help people settle in and be more present and open as we go into the meeting or activity, we have in front of us.

- *When the group is gathered, ask everyone to put down any devices and find a comfortable position*
- *Invite everyone to close their eyes and turn their attention inwards. Ask them to notice what unfinished business they are mentally carrying with them into this gathering. What thoughts, emotions or other things are*

*being processed in their minds, that have nothing to do with what you are going to do together?*

- *Ask participants, to their best ability, to park whatever they have noticed in a mental parking lot, agreeing with themselves that they will come back to their unresolved issues later.*
- *Now, invite them to notice where they are right now. Ask them to notice the chair they are sitting in and what it feels like, where their feet rest on the floor. As they notice their body, invite them to allow their body to relax.*
- *Ask them to notice their breathing and see if their shoulders can sink down a bit more with every outbreath.*
- *Finally, ask participants to tune in to the topic for your gathering. Why are you here?*
- *Invite them to reflect on what they hope to accomplish with this meeting. What would a good outcome be?*
- *Pose a final question for the participants to contemplate before you finish the check-in; How can you best contribute to this gathering being a success?*

Even if it can feel awkward at first to propose this kind of start to a group activity, I have frequently heard meeting participants testify that they felt so much calmer and more prepared after these few minutes. If we want to create a setting where we can be focused, open and creative together, spending a few minutes to have everyone's nervous system calm down and intentions calibrated can prove to give a good return on investment.

### Keeping the open mind – paying attention to the four levels of listening

As we touched on earlier in this chapter, the way we relate and listen to each other will influence what we will be able explore, what new perspectives we can discover and how creative we can be together.

 When in meetings, a powerful practice is to pause every now and then to notice our attitude and level of listening. We can use the following questions for our reflection:

- *Am I currently listening with the intention to answer back, or to really understand what others are sharing?*
- *What questions can I ask to help me open my own blind spots?*
- *What can I do to really understand the other person's needs and feelings around this issue?*
- *How can we make this a co-creative win-win conversation where no one needs to be right?*

As you probably can recognise, the questions relate to what Otto Scharmer calls the four levels of listening. By paying attention to how we shift back and forth between the levels, we become more aware of when we go into an unnecessary rigid or defensive position and can consciously activate curious and empathic listening again.

Building awareness like this can be done individually, but also collectively. I have often introduced the four levels of listening in groups and put them on a flipchart on the wall during more challenging processes. Every now and then during the process, we have paused and asked the group members to reflect on at what level they have been listening and interacting with each other. After a while, the group often becomes more aware of the dynamics and can self-regulate when conversations get polarised instead of curious.

### Applying the dwelling mind

As many of us have experienced, new insights and ideas don't always show up when we are working hard at our desk, but more often when we step away from our problems and do something else.

To let the subconscious regions of our brain work for us, we need to allow some time and space for connections to be made. Letting our mind dwell on an issue is a bit like slow cooking. Sometimes we need to let ingredients simmer for a while to bring out the best in them.

A practical way to do this can be to plan your work so that you allow time intervals where your subconscious mind can work on things. When you, for example, need to do some work that requires a holistic and creative approach to a problem, you can work at in steps:

- *Reflect on your aspiration. What is it you want to accomplish? What could good look like?*
- *Make sure you have read up on the facts and information you have available, so your mind has some data to work with.*
- *Instead of immediately trying to work out solutions, give yourself some mental space. Depending on the context, this can be going for a short walk where you just let your thoughts flow, going to the gym, sleeping on it, or even agreeing with yourself to get back to the problem a few days later.*
- *When thoughts that relate to your problem pop up during this time, you don't have to push them away, but you don't want to go into active problem-solving mode either. Rather let your mind simmer thoughts in the background without forcing any conclusions.*
- *When the time has come to actively reengage with the issue, it often works well to start writing down the different insights, thoughts and*

*ideas that have emerged along the way. Once you have documented them, you can start to filter, curate, and connect ideas more critically.*

By setting our intention and engaging with the available information at the start of this process, we plant seeds in our mind. These can then germinate and with a little patience we can see what ideas sprout after a few hours, days, or weeks.

### Open awareness meditation

We have addressed various forms of mindfulness and meditation earlier in this book, but in this section, it is worth highlighting a form of meditation often referred to as open awareness meditation.

In many meditation techniques we deliberately focus our attention on some kind of object, for example, our breath or body. As we covered earlier, this trains our attention muscle and can also help us settle down and relax. We can think of these techniques as a convergent process where we gather and focus our mental energy.

Open awareness meditation is more of a divergent process where we literally invite and allow all kinds of sense perceptions, emotions, thoughts, etc., to come and go, while we observe them from a place of neutral awareness. This conscious and neutral observing is what makes open awareness meditation different from daydreaming. We are not lost in thought, but rather observing our own stream of mental activities, as if we were a spectator to our own mind.

There is an interesting application here related to creativity and our ability to sense patterns in complex situations. With a little practice, open awareness meditation offers a way to let our mind flow freely, letting thoughts emerge and connections to be made, while at the same time a part of us is aware and observing. Below is an example of an open awareness meditation that you can experiment with.

- *Find a place where you can be undisturbed. If necessary, set a timer for the time you have available.*
- *Take your seat and find a position that feels both relaxed and alert at the same time.*
- *Close your eyes or let your relaxed gaze fall at a neutral place.*
- *Start by noticing your breath. No need to control it, just let your breathing flow naturally, and for a minute or so, just observe the air coming in and out.*
- *While keeping the sensation of breathing in your awareness, now also notice your body. Open to all sensations that are present in your body, clear or subtle. It can be a feeling of tension somewhere or a tingling*

*sensation of energy. You don't have to focus on any particular sensa-*
*tion, but rather open up to the cloud of different sensations that come*
*and go in your body as you sit and observe.*

- *Next, open to sensory impressions coming from the space around you,*
  *like sounds, smells, air, temperature, etc. See if you can just take the*
  *impressions in, without evaluating them or getting lost in thoughts*
  *related to them.*
- *Finally, invite your thoughts and feelings to flow freely in your mind.*
  *Like with the other objects, see if you can let them show up in your*
  *mind without grabbing on to them. Rather observe your own thoughts*
  *and feelings as if you were a spectator of your own mental activity.*
- *Allow yourself to sit with a totally open awareness where there is space*
  *for everything, breath, bodily sensations, sounds, thoughts.... Approach*
  *it as if your awareness was like a vast open sky. No matter what clouds*
  *come and go, your awareness has a spacious quality, surrounding it all.*
- *As you observe physical as well as mental experiences, notice how they*
  *are all coming and going. There are no permanent sounds, sensations,*
  *or even thoughts. Everything is in a constant flow. If you notice your*
  *mind wants to hold on to a thought or a feeling, relax and release. Let*
  *the flow continue as you just hold it in awareness.*
- *When your timer rings, or when you feel ready, gather yourself by*
  *returning your attention to your breath for a minute. Then open your*
  *eyes fully and come back.*

Like with all techniques, it takes some practice with open awareness
meditation to find the balance between being relaxed and open, and yet
present and consciously observing. Once you get the hang of it, this technique can be a helpful tool to connect to the more intuitive aspects of
our mind. Many business leaders, for example, Bridgewater hedge fund
founder Ray Dalio and former Plantronics CEO Bill George, as well as
Steve Jobs have testified to how their meditation practice has been a key to
help them see new ideas and develop their businesses.

### Using flow-writing to let patterns and ideas emerge

Another technique that links well with the dwelling mind and the open
awareness meditation is flow-writing, that we have explored earlier in the
book. As with the other practices, flow-writing aims at creating a space
where thoughts and ideas that haven't fully crystallised yet, can start to
form.

The core principle for flow-writing is not to over-think or edit before
you write things down. You would rather let all your thoughts flow out
on paper, so you can look at them afterwards. Flow-writing is a sort of a

brain-dump on paper. We invite the things that are processing in our more subconscious mind, to come out unfiltered.

This can be a helpful practice every time we feel we need to get perspectives on things, sort our own thinking or want to invite new ideas. You do not need a lot of preparation, just something to write on and some undisturbed time.

It often helps to prompt the process with some questions and sentences to get your writing going, like:

- *What is on my mind right now is...*
- *What wants to emerge is...*
- *The different perspectives on this situation are...*
- *The possibilities I can see right now are....*

As we start writing, we try to keep the pen moving as much as possible and avoid stopping and evaluating too much along the way. We want to give our inner editor a break and let as many things as possible flow out through our writing.

Once we have emptied our mind on paper, we can start looking at the result with a more analytical approach. This is where we engage our rational pre-frontal cortex, i.e. the higher regions of the brain, to filter the information. Reading through your notes, reflect on:

- *What stands out?*
- *What patterns can I see?*
- *What ideas or perspectives become clearer?*
- *What emerges that I should act on?*

Flow-writing can be used to process complex problems individually, but also in groups. Starting a meeting with a few minutes of flow-writing on a topic can be a good way to help participants tune in, get different perspectives on the table, or start a creative process.

### Creating results together with others

In this chapter, we have explored approaches and practices that can help us as individuals to better navigate complexity and uncertainty. But addressing challenging situations is seldom something we do alone. On top of the personal practices we have covered, there is a wide range of dialogue techniques, methods for facilitating group processes, etc., that also can help us tackle complex problems and lead transformational processes.

As the scope for this book is focused on the inner, personal capabilities we can cultivate as individuals, I will not go deeper into the field of creative group processes. If you are curious to explore this more, I can recommend you check out resources related to Design Thinking.[22] Other relevant resources I have referenced earlier is Peter Senge's work on learning organisations and especially The Fifth Discipline Fieldbook[23] which contains many practical tools. Otto Scharmer's book Theory U[24] also offers a wealth of practical group processes and exercises.

However, even if I have chosen to focus this book on qualities of leadership we can cultivate as individuals, this doesn't mean our focus should be just on ourselves – quite the opposite. Our work and impact are always in relation to and influencing other people. In our next chapter, we are therefore going to explore how we can cultivate personal qualities such as empathy and compassion to be more skilful and beneficial in our interactions with others.

## Notes

1  In the book *Complexity and the Experience of Leading Organizations* (2015), Stacey comments on typical leadership experiences from a complexity perspective. You can also check out a short video giving an overview of Stacey's thinking by searching for: *Ralph Stacey - Complexity and Paradoxes*. The Stacey Complexity Matrix is also a helpful tool, briefly explained in this article: praxisframework.org/en/library/stacey-matrix.

2  The Cynefin Framework is a conceptual tool to support problem solving and decision-making. It was created Dave Snowden while he worked for IBM Global Services. You can find more information and inspiration on thecynefin.co/about-us/about-cynefin-framework.

3  You can read more about Dan Siegel's work on drdansiegel.com. He is also the founder of the Mindsight Institute, offering various courses and resources: mindsightinstitute.com.

4  Daniel J. Siegel, *Mindsight: The New Science of Personal Transformation* (2005).

5  Check out his homepage davidrock.net. You can also find keynotes with David Rock on YouTube.

6  David Rock, *Your Brain at Work: Strategies for Overcoming Distraction, Regaining Focus, and Working Smarter All Day Long* (2009).

7  Under resources on Amy Edmondson's homepage amycedmondson.com/recommended-resources you can find links to interesting articles, videos and more relating to psychological safety and teaming.

8  Amy Edmondson, *The Fearless Organization: Creating Psychological Safety in the Workplace for Learning, Innovation, and Growth* (2018).

9  Serena Chen is a professor of psychology at UC Berkeley. You can explore more by searching for these articles: hbr.org/2018/09/give-yourself-a-break-the-power-of-self-compassion, J.G. Breines and S. Chen, *Self-Compassion Increases Self-Improvement Motivation* (2012). journals.sagepub.com/doi/abs/10.1177/0146167212445599.

10  Rich Hanson is neuroscientist and psychologist who offer practical tips related to happiness, well-being, and personal development. Read more about his thinking in this article on the neuroscience of happiness greatergood.berkeley.

edu/article/item/the_neuroscience_of_happiness or check out the resources on his homepage rickhanson.com.

11 You can find a lot of inspiration and resources on systemsawareness.org.

12 Yuval Noah Harari is today one of the world's best known public thinkers. He has written bestselling books like *Sapiens – A brief History of Humankind* (2011), *Homo Deus – A Brief History of Tomorrow* (2015) and *21 Lessons for the 21st Century* (2018). He is also a frequent guest in podcasts and at global conferences. ynharari.com.

13 Robert Kegan and Lisa Lahey, *Immunity to Change: How to Overcome It and Unlock the Potential in Yourself and Your Organization* (2009). I can highly recommend exploring this framework and the thinking around it. This article offers a brief introduction: gse.harvard.edu/hgse100/story/changing-better.

14 Peter Senge's work has had a strong influence on the field of systems thinking and organisational learning. Two of his most popular books are *The Fifth Discipline: The Art & Practice of The Learning Organization* (1990) and *The Fifth Discipline Fieldbook: Strategies and Tools for Building a Learning Organization* (1994). Some of his other work can be found here: mitsloan.mit.edu/faculty/directory/peter-m-senge.

15 Otto Scharmer is well known for his work on Theory U, *Theory U: Leading from the Future as It Emerges* (2009) where he presents an approach to working with change and transformation in complex systems. You can also learn more on u-school.org/theory-u. Scharmer is the founder of Presencing Institute which offers support and trainings related to working with the principles of Theory U presencinginstitute.org.

16 You can search for, *Otto Scharmer on the four levels of listening* to find videos of him explaining his version of the four levels of listening.

17 Explore systemsawareness.org.

18 Find both free resources and paid-for trainings at u-school.org and presencinginstitute.org.

19 To find an excerpt from his book *Good to Great* (2001) where Jim Collins refers to his conversation with Admiral Jim Stockdale, you can search for "Jim Collins-Concepts-Stockdale paradox".

20 Bechara et al., Science 1997: *Deciding Advantageously before Knowing the Advantageous Strategy*. science.org/doi/10.1126/science.275.5304.1293.

21 Malcolm Gladwell, *Blink: The Power of Thinking without Thinking* (2005).

22 This article introduces principles and ideas in Design Thinking mitsloan.mit.edu/ideas-made-to-matter/design-thinking-explained. Stanford d.school dschool.stanford.edu also offers various tips and resources.

23 Peter Senge, *The Fifth Discipline Fieldbook: Strategies and Tools for Building a Learning Organization* (1994).

24 Otto Scharmer, *Theory U: Leading from the Future as It Emerges* (2009).

# Chapter 4

# Collaborating across divides

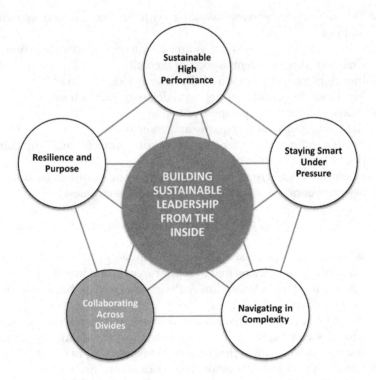

*Figure 4.1* The five areas of building sustainable leadership from the inside.

## Overview Chapter 4: Collaborating across divides

We often depend on others to create the results we aspire to, no matter if it is collaborating on a smaller project in our own department or addressing larger strategic challenges in our organisation or

DOI: 10.4324/9781003485148-5

society. But working with diverse groups of people and collaborating with those who have different approaches, beliefs, or goals then ourselves, is not always a smooth ride.

In this chapter we unpack the neurological underpinnings of empathy and inclusion, and what makes us open to other people's perspectives and willing to collaborate with them. We will explore frameworks that can help us understand the dynamics of silo thinking, exclusion and conflict, and introduce concrete practices for leveraging our ability for compassion, inclusion and collaborating across divides.

*These are some of the areas we are going to cover:*

- The difference between working with an ego vs. eco system mindset
- How empathy and trust act as lubrication in cross-collaboration
- Understanding different aspects of empathy
- In-groups vs. out-groups and the shadow side of empathy
- The inner aspects of working with diversity and inclusion
- Practices to enhance perspective taking
- Activating our innate empathy and compassion
- Understanding the deeper aspects of conflicts and difficult situations
- Leading with a strong back and a soft front – combining openness and curiosity with discernment and assertiveness

*Examples of how this part relates to and supports other sections:*

- When going into tense and difficult situations we can leverage many of the practice related to self-awareness and impulse control covered in *Staying Smart Under Pressure* as well as *Navigating in Complexity*.
- As we explore perspective taking, empathy and compassion in this part of the book, we will also see how these capabilities relate to systems understanding that we cover in *Navigating in Complexity*.
- Self-awareness and self-compassion are closely related to perspective taking, empathy and compassion for others, and all these elements play essential roles in the last part of the book related to Resilience and Purpose.

*Supporting audio material*
There are guided audio practices accompanying this chapter. Search for *Meditations for Leaders (Joakim Eriksson)* to find them on your preferred audio platform.

## The business case for empathy and compassion

Although empathy and compassion are traits that we usually would think of as positive in human beings, there can be a tendency to underestimate their importance in organisational settings or in any situations where we need to create things together with other people.

One could argue that our ability to care for other people's needs and be open to their perspectives functions as a lubrication in all kinds of collaboration. Without it, turf wars, polarisation and silo thinking can come to dominate.

As we are going to explore in this part of the book, empathy and compassion are innate capacities in us as human beings. However, they can be more or less easily available to us, depending on the context. These so called 'soft skills' can be some of the 'hardest skills' to bring into action, when we find ourselves in situations where we need to collaborate with people, we don't like a lot.

The purpose of the following sections is to unpack how empathy can influence efficiency in collaboration, how it works in the brain, and most importantly, how we can intentionally train our empathy, compassion and inclusion muscles.

## Noticing the ego and eco system mindsets at play

No matter what context we are acting in, our basic mindset toward others will influence how we interact and prioritise. To start with, I would like to introduce you to a metaphor for how we can approach collaboration with others.

Otto Scharmer, who I have mentioned earlier, came up with the expression ego system vs. eco system approach to describe two very different mindsets that can be applied to an organisational or societal context. When an organisation operates from an *ego system* mindset, members of the organisation put most of their focus on what is important for their own department or unit. Members are still aware that they are a part of a bigger picture, but on a daily basis, money, time and resources are mainly spent on optimising their own unit's goals.

If the same organisation would operate from an *eco system* mindset, each unit would still have their separate skill sets and areas of responsibility, but there would be much more focus on how different units can work together to contribute to the overall mission of the organisation. Even if the organisation is divided into smaller units for practical purposes, these units are focused on sharing information, resources, etc., between each other to support the greater whole.

For years, I have asked leaders to reflect on what mindset dominates in their organisation, and a vast majority of them testify that the ego system mindset seems to have the upper hand. Organisational structures, but also budgets and incentive systems seem to support a more divided approach to work inside organisations. At the same time, many leaders say that in order to tackle the real strategic challenges their organisation is facing, they would need to work more along the lines of an eco system approach.

Based on this, we may think that the eco system approach is the right answer in all situations. I would personally like to argue that prioritising the bigger picture is always a good thing, but it can also be helpful to be pragmatic and nuanced here. Let us say that an organisation functions in a way where the different departments and units have low interdependence, i.e. they can operate well separately with little need for help from, or contact with, each other, the ego system approach might be the most effective way. There is less need for meetings and alignment between people. As long as all separate units do their job, they can deliver the required parts or results to the mother organisation, and everyone is happy.

However, in an organisation where the different units depend on each other to succeed with their goals, the ego approach can become problematic. This can, for example, often be the case when an organisation faces complex challenges that require departments to co-create solutions to problems they haven't met before. In these conditions, units may have to shift more to an eco system approach, let go of their focus on separate goals and focus on what they need to solve together as an organisation. The Covid-19 crisis brought out this shift in mindset and level of collaboration in many organisations, for example, in the health care sector.

In invite you to reflect on how you experience these dynamics in your own life:

- *What mindset would you say dominate in the organisation you work in?*
- *Is it context dependent?*
- *In what situations are ego or eco approaches used?*
- *Is this choice of approach a conscious one, or just a part of the culture and way of working?*
- *When you look into the future, do you think you will need more ego or eco approaches?*

Instead of thinking of the ego vs. eco system approaches as right or wrong, it is more useful to ask ourselves if we are applying the right approach in the right situation. My experience from 30+ years in organisational life tells me that the ego system approach tends to dominate in organisations, also in situations where it isn't helpful. I also sense that more and more organisations are facing situations that call for an eco system approach.

By starting to reflect on our basic attitude and approach (do we instinctively act as if we are separate entities or as parts of a bigger whole?), we open up for a more conscious approach to collaboration. The following sections will focus on how we can be more efficient agents for an eco system approach. To work with that mindset requires us to cultivate empathy, perspective taking and a sense of connecting with others.

## Trust and connection as lubrication for collaboration

When we find ourselves in situations of interdependence, i.e. that we depend on others to create the results we want, the quality of our relations becomes the lubrication for effective collaboration.

The feeling of trust between us and the people we work with is one such lubricator. We all have our own experiences of situations where there has been a high level of trust between people and how that has made it easier to solve difficult issues. And we have most likely experienced the opposite when the lack of trust makes collaboration more difficult, energy draining, and time consuming.

If we break down the experience of trust into smaller elements, we can see that parts of what build it has to do with to what degree we experience others to be credible, trustworthy, and reliable. This is often related to their skills, competencies, discipline, etc. But there are other more subtle elements that also influence trust.

When we feel that other people truly care for us and bother to understand our needs and perspectives, it builds connection. When we learn more about other people and what is important in their life, the sense of connection grows. Edgar Schein, a thought leader in the field of organisational culture and leadership points to how the quality of personal relations influences organisational effectiveness. In his work,[1] Schein often refers to different levels of relations, along these lines:

- Negative and hostile relations
- Polite, professional, and transactional relations
- Personal relations where people relate to each other as individuals
- Private relations and friendships

Schein's research has indicated that personal relationships often bring about the most effective collaboration. People don't necessarily have to be friends, but they can relate to each other as individuals and have respect and understanding for each other's needs. In many organisations, relationships at the purely professional and transactional level can work well in certain settings but they seem to put a limitation on the potential for real trust and co-creation. More close and private relations at work can on the other hand become problematic as it can create barriers for tackling difficult situations in objective and constructive ways.

The bottom line is that we don't have to share private details with each other at work or become close friends with our colleagues. But, if we want to build the capability to work effectively together on complex and difficult problems, research indicates that it helps to drop our professional masks every now and then and show a genuine interest in each other as human beings.

Take a moment to reflect on what level of relation you have with some of your key stakeholders and colleagues:

- *How would you rate your level of relation according to the definitions above?*
- *How much do you know about the person, beyond their professional role?*
- *What do you know about their personal interests, drivers, and motivations?*
- *How much have you shared with them about yourself?*
- *What level of relation would be most helpful for your collaboration?*

## Psychological safety – a key denominator in high-performing teams

A term that sometimes is used to describe open and trusting relationships is *psychological safety*. In a large multi-year research project on team effectiveness at Google called Project Aristoteles,[2] one of the key findings was that the psychological safety was a common denominator among high-performing teams. Amy Edmondson at Harvard has also dedicated much of her research into this phenomenon, well described in her book *The Fearless Organization*.[3] It seems that in environments where we sense that it is safe to make a mistake, and people around us will help us rather than use it against us, we lean it, give more of ourselves and collaborate better.

I sometimes call psychological safety the cousin of trust, just to indicate that these two phenomena are related but not exactly the same. Building trust between people is often a process that takes time and is closely related to their personal relation. Psychological safety however, can arguably be established between people who have never met before, by setting a clear context and working according to certain ground rules.

What lays the foundation for psychological safety as well as trust is the willingness to be open and vulnerable and to show a genuine interest in helping others. When we sense that these elements are present, we tend to bring the best of ourselves to a collaboration. To refer to the first chapter in this book, feeling safe lowers our stress levels and gives us easier access to the parts of our brain related to creativity and big picture thinking.

## Leveraging diversity and working with true inclusion

Trust and psychological safety are also closely related to the topics of diversity and inclusion. Over the last decades there has been an increasing focus on, and research into, diversity, equality, and inclusion and how it influences the effectiveness of organisations and functioning of societies.

Besides the foundational ethical reasons for promoting more diversity, equality and inclusion, research has also shown that it is good business. Organisations that work consciously with these topics show higher resilience in the face of challenges, better decision making, more innovation, etc.

For good reasons, a lot of focus in the movement for more diversity, equality and inclusion, has been put on gender, ethnicity, and sexual orientation. However, we should not limit our understanding of diversity and inclusion to these areas, but also look beyond. In human interactions there can be many other, sometimes very subtle, markers that make us dismiss or exclude people we sense are different from themselves. These dividers can be related to neuro diversity, educational or sociodemographic background, areas of professional expertise, political views, etc.

Inviting diversity for real, requires us to constantly challenge our own comfort and ask ourselves how we can bring in the voices and perspectives we ourselves might be blind to and even find irritating. Truly working with inclusion requires us to stay open and curious when people express the 'wrong' views.

Working with diversity and inclusion is not a smooth ride. Engaging with people who differ from ourselves will inevitably trigger reactions that are hard-wired into us human beings by evolution. But just because it is difficult, it does not mean that we shouldn't engage in it – quite the contrary.

Because some of the underlying and subconscious mental processes that drive exclusion, discrimination and polarisation are so deeply ingrained in us, we constantly need to pay attention, grow our awareness and do what we can to upgrade our mental 'operating systems'. When we do this, it opens the door to possibilities to collaborate and co-create in larger and larger contexts, and address more complex challenges together. By recognising how we as individuals, groups and organisations all have our own biases and blind spots, we can get better at recognising them and work more skilfully with them.

Part of addressing issues related to diversity, equality and inclusion is to work with structural changes. This can be anything from legislation to an organisation's policy on parental leave or the design of recruitment processes.

Thankfully there is much good advice and guidance available today on what can be done to improve structures and processes in this regard.

But no matter what structures we put into place, the inner place from which each individual thinks and acts will also influence the outcome. In this chapter on collaborating across divides, we will therefore look at the inner aspects of inclusion such as empathy and compassion, which we all can cultivate as individuals, and which will determine what mindset we will apply and how we will use structures and processes in real life.

## Understanding empathy and compassion

Empathy and compassion are terms we use in our daily language, but we may have different understandings of what the terms entail. Not that a formal definition is important in itself, but for the following sections to make most sense, it can be helpful to have a shared reference point.

The way we refer to empathy here has nothing to do with feeling sorry for, agreeing with, or giving in to other people. It is fully possible to have different points of views and even take tough decisions that other people disagree with, while still being empathetic. One formal definition of empathy is:

> *The ability to experience and understand what others feel, while maintaining a clear discernment about your own and the other person's feelings and perspectives.*[4]

In the coming chapter, we are going to unpack different aspects of empathy and how they influence our interactions with others.

### Three aspects of empathy

In literature on psychology empathy is sometimes being split up into different categories, which are quite helpful to understand how empathy plays out in our lives. Three main categories often described are:

- **Cognitive empathy** – the ability to intellectually understand other people's perspectives, needs and feelings. For example, if a colleague of ours gets fired or we see someone falling on a street, scratching their knees, we can cognitively understand that these must be unpleasant experiences for the people involved.

  Cognitive empathy is what we use when we practice perspective taking, and are able to intellectually entertain and reflect on different points of view.
- **Emotional or affective empathy** – the ability to actually feel and experience what other people are feeling. We can sense the feelings of grief and

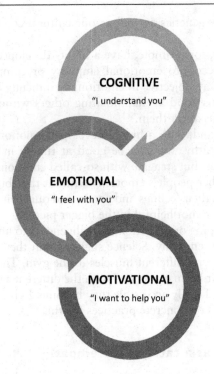

*Figure 4.2* Three aspects of empathy.

uncertainty of the colleagues who lost their jobs, or the pain associated with scratched knees.

Emotional empathy engages our so-called mirror neurons that pick up on other people's feelings and moods, and trigger the same emotional reactions in us. This is what makes us influenced by other people's emotions and helps us relate more deeply to what it means to be in the other persons' situation.

- **Motivational empathy,** also referred to as **Compassion,** is the drive to want to help others relieve their suffering. We can think of compassion as adding action to empathy. When we feel compassion, we not only relate to other people's situation, but we feel a natural urge to help them. This drive to help is the key differentiator between empathy and compassion.

As we probably have experienced in our own life, we can have more or less easily access to these different aspects of empathy. Contemporary neuroscience has identified that these three different aspects actually correlate with different networks in our brain,[5] which can be more or less developed in us. Research suggests that how easily we access empathy can be influenced both by genetics as well as our cultural conditioning and personal experiences.

Some of us can, for example, have a highly developed cognitive empathy, while little access to emotional empathy or compassion. This can make it easier to stay objective in emotionally difficult situations, but also potentially make us good at manipulating others without much concern for how our actions affect them.

On the other hand, with a highly developed emotional resonance and low cognitive empathy, we may be good at tuning in to other people's emotions and needs, but struggle with so-called emotional contamination, i.e. we take on other people's emotions without the ability to discern the difference between their feelings and needs, and our own. This too can lead to behaviors that are not helpful in the bigger picture.

A key to developing our emotional intelligence is to understand and cultivate all aspects of empathy. Science suggests that they can all be trained like we would exercise different muscles in the gym. The more we engage the networks in our brain associated with the different aspects of empathy, the more active and easily accessible they become. In later sections we will go into more depth on concrete practices for this.

## Self-awareness as a catalyst for empathy

An underestimated influence on our empathic abilities is our own self-awareness. The neural networks engaged in monitoring and understanding other people are the same as those activated when we interpret our own mental states.[6] In a sense, we can only recognise mental states in others, we can relate to ourselves.

I have met many leaders that pride themselves with putting their own feelings aside in order to be professional at work. This might have the best intentions, but the shadow side of this approach is that numbing down their own emotional signals risks making them insensitive to cues from other people as well. As a core part of leadership is to monitor and facilitate the energy, motivation, and well-being of a team, shutting down our empathic capacities can lead to dysfunctional work environments.

On the other hand, leaders who cultivate their ability to observe and get familiar with their own emotions, feelings and thought processes, can more easily pick up on other people's emotions and understand other's experiences. The self-awareness practices we explored earlier in the book, are therefore a helpful foundation for cultivating our empathic capabilities.

## The origins of empathy and its shadow side

As mentioned before, genetical predisposition and cultural conditioning can influence our general level of empathy. Besides that, there are more fluent factors that also will determine to what degree our ability for empathy will actually come into play in our daily life.

Empathy is an innate mental function in primates in general but is especially well developed in humans. Evolutionary psychologists point to how this ability to care for the needs of other individuals outside our closest family circle, has played a unique role in the way humans have been able to operate in larger tribes and build societies.

Empathy was a mental function that enabled early humans to collaborate in larger numbers than many other species. For example, to organise a tribe into smaller groups where some hunted, some collected eatable plants and some guarded all the children, and then share what had been gathered between themselves, required trusting and caring for each other. Early humans that leveraged this mental capacity became better at collaborating effectively and had a bigger chance for survival. Over the millennia, evolution has rewarded empathy and compassion, and enabled us to build larger societies, nations as well as multinational organisations where we relate to, care for, and help each other to thrive.

However, there is also a shadow side to the evolutionary roots of empathy. These traits developed to help and protect those we considered to be part of our tribe. But, if we encountered someone not belonging to our tribe, we could be dismissive or even violent toward them, as they might be competing for our food or even be a threat to us.

We could say that our innate empathy, developed by evolution, comes with a 'bug' we need to be aware of. We have a natural ability to understand, feel for, and want to help other people. But these empathic abilities generally only activate if we sense that other people are similar to us. This bug is what underpins a lot of exclusive behavior, protectionism and even racism we can see in our societies.

## The dynamics of in-groups and out-groups

Although humans have developed a lot since we were living in tribes on the savannah, some basic instincts still rule how our brain works. One of these is that subconscious parts of our mind always scan people we encounter, trying to answer the questions "who is part of my tribe". Our minds want to quickly place others in either our in-group or out-group, to be able to determine how to relate toward them.

In a thought-provoking experiment by David Eagleman and his team,[7] a group of volunteers were put in a functional MR-scanner that could register brain activity in real time. The subjects were then shown a video of a hand getting stabbed by a needle, which provoked a neural response in the pain center in their own brain. This is a sign of normal functioning emotional empathy – we can feel what other people feel.

Then the researchers changed the videos slightly, adding a single word next to the hand getting stabbed; Muslim, Christian, Atheist, etc.

The results indicated a clear pattern; when subjects watched a hand get stabbed with a label of the same religion as the subject, their brains registered an immediate empathic response. But, when watching someone belonging to another religion getting stabbed, their brain hardly reacted.

This uncovers a not-so-pretty part of how our human minds work. Our brain's pre-conscious response to another person in pain seems to depend on whether we believe they belong to the same group as us, or not. And for the record, atheists reacted the same way as people identifying as religious, so it doesn't seem to have to do with religion per se. Similar experiments have been performed in other labs using other differentiators such as what sports team you support or what political party you belong to.

The bottom line here is that when our mind, consciously or subconsciously, labels another person as different from us, the way we relate to them will shift. We are less likely to pay attention to their needs, listen to their point of view or offer them help.

### Cultivating awareness of how we construct our in- and out-groups

It can be embarrassing to admit to ourselves that our brains constantly label others either a part of our in- or out-group. There is good news here though. By becoming aware of this innate function of our brain, we can start to nudge it toward a more inclusive default mode.

The way our minds define the in-group is very fluid and context dependent. Let us take the example of football supporters. I certain cities, rivaling supporters can literally fight each other based on the single factor that they support different teams. The same people can then show up at a national team event, and in this context, they support the same team – their national team. The context has changed, and they now identify themselves as being part of the same in-group.

We can use this plasticity of our mind to cultivate a more inclusive approach. Over time, we can increase the variety of people our mind will interpret as part of our in-group. The key here is often the language we use. In my work as an organisational consultant, I get to visit and work with a wide variety of companies and organisations. One of the things I always listen for when I start to work with leaders and team members is who they talk about as 'us' in the organisation, and who they call 'them'. This subtle difference indicates where they draw boundaries of their in-groups.

Often this use of language is not conscious, but over time, the words we use will create our mental reality. Especially if we have a leadership role or any position of authority, how we speak about, for example, other departments and label them as an in-group or out-group, will influence how our colleagues will relate to them.

Take a moment to reflect on this yourself:

- *Who do you refer to as 'us' and 'them' when you talk about colleagues and stakeholders?*
- *What makes you draw the distinction between them the way you do?*
- *How do you think your labeling influences the way you relate to them?*
- *If you were to formulate yourself more consciously, how would you adapt your language?*

Silo thinking, polarisation and turf wars are responsible for a lot of wasted energy, time and money in organisations, and the roots of these behaviors are often unchecked biases and lack of reflection on how we have created our mental in- and out-groups. But we are not bad people because our brains do this labeling, we are just humans. We can be caring and loving people, and still do unhelpful or even bad things to people that our subconscious mind has labelled as being outside our circle of concern. By paying attention and nudging our minds toward more inclusive in-group definitions, we can rise above our more primitive instincts, and be more effective when collaborating with diverse groups of people.

## Approaching others with a heart at war or a heart at peace

The conscious or subconscious dividing of others into in/out-groups is possibly the strongest influencer on our attitude toward them and thereby how effective we will be in building relations and collaborating. But even with people who we consider to be in our in-group, like close colleagues or family members, we can still get triggered and become defensive, rigid, and even hostile.

As we explored in Chapter 2 of this book around self-awareness and self-leadership, our brain tends to shut down much of our empathic functions when we are upset, feel threatened or mistreated. To be able to collaborate with people that trigger us or to work constructively to solve an ongoing conflict, we need to be able to step out of our mental self-defense positions.

In their book *The Anatomy of Peace*,[8] the Arbinger Institute describes this as approaching a situation with a heart at peace rather than a heart at war. They have studied and worked with conflict resolution for decades and point to how our inner state and attitude toward others will influence how effective our interventions will be.

When we do the objectively 'right' things with an underlying aggressive or judgmental attitude, the receiving party will sense it and respond accordingly. On the other hand, if we sense genuine openness and curiosity from others, we tend to lower our own mental guard and engage more willingly in problem solving.

One of the aspirations of this book you hold in your hand is to offer practices for cultivating a 'heart of peace', so we can do whatever action we do from a place in ourselves that is as clear, open, and well-intended as possible. We cannot control the attitude and behaviors of others, but by nurturing a heart of peace in ourselves, we can influence others toward a more open attitude and create the foundation for more effective collaborations.

## The inner work of inclusion – practices for activating empathy and making our in-groups larger

In the following sections we will introduce a series of concrete practices, designed to activate the circuits in our brain related to the different aspects of empathy we have covered. Metaphorically, we can see these practices as exercise machines in an empathy gym. They train our ability to take other people's perspectives, sense what other people are feeling, expand our in-groups and cultivate our natural inclination to help others.

Embedded in these practices are two core elements that have been shown to activate and cultivate our empathy and compassion:

- To actively look for the similarities between ourselves and others
- To offer kindness, in form of an act or even just a thought

There is nothing mystical about these practices. To draw a parallel to physical training, we know that when we activate certain muscle groups on a regular basis, they work better. When we do certain physical movements on a regular basis, for example, dancing or playing an instrument, our body will remember the movements, and over time we can do them with more ease and skill.

The following examples of empathy practices work the same way. By deliberately activating our cognitive, emotional, and motivational empathy, these mental abilities get fired up and are more readily available to us. Hence, they will grow into natural habits of our minds.

### Bubble hopping

The first practice focuses on perspective taking and has been developed and used at Stockholm School of Economics to teach undergraduates and graduates to expand their understanding of the world and the needs of different groups in society.[9]

The term bubble hopping originally comes from a former Google engineer, Max Hawkins, who now works on creating algorithms that can help us break out of the filter and information bubbles created by technology. As we have discussed earlier, even without technology, our upbringing, education, and social life has a tendency to bring us into 'bubbles' where we meet and interact with people similar to us, and who tend to confirm our views. Hence, bubble hopping is a way to help ourselves out of those bubbles, if only for a moment.

The process practiced at Stockholm School of Economics is based on a few steps and principles:

### Identify persons or groups you struggle to understand

In the case of the graduates, these persons could be representatives from less privileged groups in society, people living in rural areas, religious leaders from different traditions, gang members, etc.

In an organisational context, this could instead be representatives from another business unit, potential clients or other stakeholders. The point here is to identify groups or people who you may have strong opinions about, but actually know very little about.

### Invite them for lunch

Next step is to reach out and invite a relevant person from the group for a meeting. Clarify your intention and that the sole purpose of the meeting is for you to learn and better understand their experiences and views.

In the SSE experiment, students were instructed to invite a person for a two-hour lunch meeting at a place the invited person would choose.

### Just listen and learn

This might be the trickiest part. During the meeting, you are just supposed to ask questions and listen to the other person's perspectives. No matter how much you might disagree, your role during this meeting is not to argue or share your views, just simply stay open and curious.

No matter how different you may be from each other, part of the practice is also to try to see where you can find similarities at one level or the other, between you and the other person.

### Reflect to update your own mental model

After the encounter, you are to take some time to let what you have learned sink in. There will surely be things you have heard that you will still disagree with but the idea is to see if you can combine this discernment with a willingness on your part to adjust your own point of view.

Here you can reflect on what you have seen, heard and learned that invites you to nuance or update your view on a situation. What blind spots may you have detected that call for further investigation?

Bubble hopping is a practical way to put the core principles of openness, curiosity, and empathy into action. The graduates at Stockholm School of Economics were asked to do this on a regular basis during their studies. You can, of course, choose how often and when it is relevant to do it. But making a habit of visiting other 'bubbles' and practicing openness and curiosity toward people who may be very different from us is good exercise for our empathic capabilities.

### Empathy mapping

A practice that connects well with bubble hopping is so-called empathy mapping. This technique is often used in the context of design thinking, when developing ideas for new business models or other situations where we need to better understand a target group, client, or stakeholder.

The typical questions to work with when doing an empathy map are, for example:

- *What does the other group see from their perspective?*
- *What does this group hear from their stakeholders?*
- *What is it this group experience, think and feel?*
- *What actions and behaviors do you observe from this group, and what does that tell you?*
- *What does this group struggle with?*
- *What is important to them? What are their needs and hopes?*

An empathy map helps you reflect on how another person or group perceives the world and what is important for them. It often helps to work visually with an empathy map, and you can find various useful templates to download from the net, one of the best ones developed by David Gray at Xplane.[10]

The map can be used to summarise impressions after having done bubble hopping, visited a client or interviewed a stakeholder. The empathy map can also be used to spark a brainstorm session or as a reflection tool for yourself, even without visiting or interviewing the person you would like to understand better. In this case, you go through the questions and just try to imagine yourself in the shoes of the other person.

By working through the different sections and questions on the map, you help yourself to connect more deeply to different aspects of another person's situation. This activates the empathy circuits in our brain and helps us to connect to them, even if we do not have all the facts. Reflecting with the help of an empathy map will probably also uncover how much we don't know about the other person or group. This can invite some humility around our own assumptions, and hopefully spark a genuine curiosity to learn more directly from the other persons.

## Compassion practices

Variations of the following visualisation practices have been used for millennia in spiritual traditions to evoke compassion. Contemporary research has confirmed that these kinds of practices, even when done in totally secular contexts, have positive effects on the well-being of the practitioners, as well as inspires more helpful and altruistic behaviors.

### The personal benefits of compassion practices

There are many relational benefits to cultivating empathy, but as we touched on earlier, taking in other people's feelings can in some situations lead to an experience of emotional overload. As a way to subconsciously protect ourselves, we can therefore sometimes 'shut down' our empathy and distance ourselves from other people's needs.

Studies by Tania Singer and Olga Klimecki, leading researchers on empathy and compassion, have shown that there is a subtle but important difference between emotional empathy and compassion (previously also referred to as motivational empathy). When we activate emotional empathy, our brain will mirror the feelings of other people. If the people we are relating to are experiencing pain or suffering, we will experience similar emotions in our own nervous system, which can wear us down over time, a phenomenon known as empathy fatigue. Compassion on the other hand, has been shown to activate networks in the brain linked to reward systems and pro-social behavior.[11]

As you may remember, the key difference compared to empathy is that compassion includes actively engaging the intention of helping. When our compassion circuitry is activated, levels of emotional stress are reduced and motivation to act is increased. It seems like the reward systems in our brain are hard-wired in a way that makes us feel good when we offer kindness and act with the intention of helping others. This makes compassion practices a powerful coping strategy when we find ourselves in difficult situations or are exposed to people who are suffering.

The Dalai Lama, spiritual leader of Tibetan Buddhism and also very engaged in the scientific research on human flourishing, often points to compassion as a uniting principle across different religions as well as secular ethical practices. He likes to state:

*If you want others to be happy, practice compassion.*
*If you want to be happy yourself, practice compassion.*

His statement is backed up by more than a decade of research in both psychology and neuroscience, indicating that activating feelings of compassion both can reduce our own stress, make us relate to others with more openness and be more willing to collaborate, also with people we find difficult. Compassion practices seem to be a practical way to switch from a heart at war, to a heart at peace.

For many of us, the idea of doing dedicated mental exercises on compassion can seem foreign and awkward. I would recommend you experiment with it, nevertheless. From my own experience, doing these kinds of practices, especially when experiencing conflicts or emotionally challenging situations, has really helped me find a more open stance, see things more clearly and approach difficult conversations more skilfully.

Below are two examples of compassion practices. The core idea of these visualisation exercises is to prime our brain toward perspective taking, empathy and compassion.

### Just like me-practice

- *Find a room where you can sit/lie down comfortably and undisturbed for approximately ten minutes.*
- *You may have your eyes closed or your gaze directed slightly downwards toward something neutral.*
- *Take a few deep breaths and allow the body to relax.*
- *When you feel ready, you can turn your thoughts toward people you have contact with in your everyday life.*
- *Begin with bringing to mind a person with whom you have a good relationship.*

  - *Reflect for a moment on what is important to this person.*
  - *What do you have in common? In what way are you similar?*
  - *What is this person struggling with right now? What does he/she need?*
  - *Imagine you could help – how would this person react if you offered to help?*
  - *How would this feel to you?*
- *Now turn your thoughts to a person with whom you have a neutral relationship.*

- *Imagine what might be important to this person in her/his life*
- *What do you have in common? In what way are you similar?*
- *What is this person struggling with right now? What does he/she need?*
- *Imagine you could help – how would this person react if you offered to help?*
- *How would it feel for you to reach out and offer help?*

- *Finally, bring to mind a person with whom you have a difficult relationship.*

  - *Imagine what might be important to this person in his/her life.*
  - *Regardless of whether you feel like you are very different from this person, what do you also have in common? In what way are you similar?*
  - *Just like you have your struggles, what may this person be struggling with right now? What does he/she need?*
  - *Imagine you could help – how would this person react if you offered to help?*
  - *How would it feel for you to offer help without expecting anything in return?*

- *Now imagine that you see all the different people you have been thinking of in front of you.*

  - *What do they have in common? In what ways are they similar to each other as people?*
  - *How does it feel to think of yourself as a person who can offer them help?*
  - *Note how you are feeling right now.*

- *End the exercise by taking a few deep breaths, open your eyes and come back.*

### Offering kindness-practice

- *Begin with turning your attention inwards, noticing your body and your breathing.*
- *Allow yourself to relax a little bit more with each outbreath.*
- *See if you can find a place in your body that feels relaxed, calm and stable, and let your attention rest there for a minute.*
- *Now turn your thoughts to someone with whom you have a positive and easy relationship.*
- *Imagine the person in front of you and how you send feelings of warmth, kindness, and generosity toward this person.*

- *With this person in your mind, try saying the following sentences silently to yourself.*

  - *May you be well*
  - *May you find the true sources of happiness*
  - *May you feel safe and protected*
  - *May you find inner peace*
  - *May you experience love and connection*

    *(You can choose to replace these sentences with others that feel more natural to you. The important thing is that you can put your genuine intention into them)*

- *After this, you can turn your thoughts toward someone else you are in contact with, but with whom you may have a more neutral relationship. In the same way as before, you can silently say the sentences with this person in mind.*

  - *May you be well*
  - *May you find the true sources of happiness*
  - *May you feel safe and protected*
  - *May you find inner peace*
  - *May you experience love and connection*

    *(You can also choose to replace these sentences with others that feel more natural to you)*

- *If you currently have a conflict with someone, you can also choose to repeat the same exercise with this person in mind. This can be more challenging, but try to see what happens.*

  - *May you be well*
  - *May you find the true sources of happiness*
  - *May you feel safe and protected*
  - *May you find inner peace*
  - *May you experience love and connection*

- *You can finish this practice by directing warmth and kindness to all people, remembering to include yourself in this. Silently but with sincerity saying to yourself:*

  - *May we all be well*
  - *May we all find the true sources of happiness*
  - *May we all feel safe and protected*
  - *May we all find inner peace*
  - *May we all experience love and connection*

- *When you have directed your warmth and kindness to all the people you want, turn your attention back to yourself.*

- *How does it feel in your body now?*
- *Can you sense if something has changed in you, mentally or physically, during the exercise?*

- *End the exercise by taking a few deep breaths, open your eyes and come back.*

Doing compassion practices can generate positive experiences, and potentially help to relieve difficult emotions. However, the goal not necessarily to get rid of all difficult emotions, but to cultivate our ability to be with challenging situations without becoming defensive, polarising, or projecting blame on others. Compassion practices is a way of exploring how we can nudge and develop the way in which we are relating to others. By intentionally evoking feelings of empathy and compassion, we prime our minds toward being more open and willing to help and collaborate with others.

### Cultivating empathy and curiosity in daily conversations

There are ample opportunities to practice an empathic approach in situations we encounter on a daily basis. The conversations we have with colleagues, family members, etc., are such an arena. Below are a few examples of how we can consciously activate empathy and turn up our level of openness, curiosity and compassion.

#### Listening without interrupting or intervening

In an everyday conversation it is common that we inject comments or questions as another person is speaking. This can be relevant and add to a positive dynamic in a conversation, but it can also take the conversation in a different direction than the person you are talking to actually intended.

A way to train ourselves to stay open and curious to what someone else is trying to convey, is to intentionally listen to the other person without interrupting, i.e. wait until the other person seems to have finished, and then let a few seconds pass before you respond. As you try to listen fully, notice the natural urge to interrupt and if there is an internal commentary going on inside your mind as you remain silent.

#### Looping back what you heard the other person say

When you sense the other person has shared what they wanted to say, instead of immediately responding with your point of view, offer to loop back what you heard her/him say. This could sound something like:

*I just want to be sure that I understand you correctly. What I hear you say is….*

This helps you integrate the other person's message, shows them that you have listened, and gives him or her a chance to correct or nuance something that was intended differently from how you heard it.

### Mirroring what you experience with the other person

Besides looping back <u>what</u> you hear the person say, you can take your listening one step further by also noticing <u>how</u> they say it. Can you notice differences in the tone of voice when they talk about different subjects? What signals do you get from their body language? What can you notice about their emotional state?

As with looping back what you heard, you can also, when appropriate, offer to share the other signals you noted. As this can feel a bit more personal, you must be sensible to the situation and what relationship you have with the person, so it doesn't feel intimidating. Done skilfully, mirroring the more subtle messages a person sends can show that you really have been paying attention to them.

### Respectfully offering your perspectives

In most conversations it would be natural that you too share your point of view, ideas, or arguments. By having listened carefully and checked that you have understood what the other person wanted to convey, it is more likely that you can add your perspectives in a way that is constructive for your conversation.

When we have a clear sense of another person's point of view and can understand their background and intention, it is often easier to find the core elements where we may disagree, as well as to see what we agree on, and can build on to find solutions. This is the difference compared to what can be called 'competing monologues', i.e. where both parties are focused on getting their own points through without listening to one another.

As part of training our openness, we can be conscious of any tendency to directly confront or argue against the other person's view. This typically sounds like; "I hear what you say, <u>but</u>...". Instead we can practice to rephrase this as; "I hear what you say, <u>and</u>...".

These nuances in attitude and phrasing can shift a conversation from a 'win-over' to a 'win-win' dynamic where we cultivate a sense of respect, curiosity, and co-creative approach.

Besides cultivating more creative conversations, listening, and responding to other people in line with the principles we have explored above, can also create a sense of safe and supportive space between us, i.e. what we earlier referred to as psychological safety. The way we choose to be there as a listening partner, curbing our own need to be heard or to be right, can be a powerful contribution to building trust between us and others.

## Approaching the difficult situations

A natural element of working together with others is inevitably disagreements, tension, and sometimes open conflicts. In the previous chapter, we defined 'creative tension' as an indication of a gap between our aspirations and current reality. We also discussed that there potentially is a lot of constructive energy in this tension, but it can also be turned into frustration if not handled skilfully.

Tension between people is a sort of energy too, indicating that we are not aligned in our view of things or in what we pursue as goals. This energy can be very destructive, but potentially also used to bring a relationship to the next level of openness and trust. What seems like a barrier can potentially become an important turning point in a collaboration, if we handled it well. Most of us probably have experiences of how a resolved conflict has led to a deeper relationship.

We could argue that conflicts and disagreements are the moments of truth where we must work hard to bring out the best in us and live our values. The challenging moments are where the rubber meets the road, and we must leverage our self-awareness, self-leadership, empathy, and perspective taking.

Luckily that are many good and useful methodologies for working with and resolving conflicts with other people. In the context of this book, we will not go deeper into mediation or dialogue techniques, but rather focus on how to nurture an inner state and attitude that creates a foundation for having constructive dialogues and co-creation. We will explore two approaches that can be used for getting ourselves into a mental position where we can act with more curiosity and openness in difficult situations.

### Becoming aware of the story we are telling ourselves

Brené Brown,[12] a research professor at the University of Houston, has spent decades studying human relations and especially courage, vulnerability, and leadership. In her book *Dare to Lead*,[13] she shares what she calls *rumbling tools*, i.e. principles for handling the messiness that is part of working together with others. When finding ourselves upset or in a conflict, one of Brown's favourite tools is to use a simple sentence to help us get a perspective to the situation:

*The story I am telling myself right now, is....*

Completing this simple sentence, with some self-compassion, clarity, and honesty, can help us notice if our mind has taken us on a ride, disconnecting us from reality.

Our emotional reactions in tense and difficult situations may be motivated, but they can potentially also be disproportional. Our interpretation of a situation may be influenced by previous experiences and biases, making us climb up the ladder of inference and making assumptions. Brené Brown's simple one-liner can act as a reminder to step out of the narrative we are caught in and take a more objective view before we speak and act.

It can sometimes be helpful to share with others what story is playing in our mind. This could sound like; "I find myself reacting right now, in a way that may not be totally objective. The story I am telling myself is...".

Of course, this requires a certain level of trust and openness between the people involved. The core point here is to have the courage to verbalise the fact that everyone involved is making up a story in their own mind. When we are willing to face that, take responsibility for our own story, and at the same time know that our story is not necessarily the full truth of a situation, we can more easily be open to the fact that others may have different perspectives.

Cultivating our ability to become aware of the story we are telling ourselves, also in the heat of difficult situations, requires us to pull on many of the personal capabilities we have covered earlier in the book, like having a high level of awareness of our mental models, noticing our early warning signs, pausing our autopilot, etc. But once we have grown our ability to create that pause of self-awareness before we act on our emotions, we are much better positioned to handle difficult situations skilfully.

### Structures of difficult conversations

There is always more to a disagreement or difficult situation than meets the eye. To understand more deeply what drives tension or a conflict, it can be helpful to explore its multiple aspects.

Back in 1979, Harvard University started a research project called the Harvard Negotiation Project[14] to study and develop methods for dealing with conflicts and negotiations. Over the decades, their research covered areas ranging from global negotiations between nations, to court cases and couples counseling. Many of their key findings are laid out in the book, *Difficult Conversations*,[15] which I can highly recommend for anyone who wants to develop the ability to turn challenging conversations into learning conversations. In their book, the authors Stone, Patton, and Heen, argue that all difficult situations share some common structures. By understanding and decoding these structures, we can approach and handle situations more skilfully.

Inspired by the work of the Harvard Negotiation Project, I have over the years introduced leaders to a simple reflection exercise I call the conflict iceberg that many have found to be useful to nurture a more curious and nuanced approach to the various conflict situations they experience in their work. Although this practice doesn't match all the aspects and tools presented in the book *Difficult Conversations*, it can be an inspiration and a starting point for a different approach to a challenging situation.

### Exploring the conflict iceberg

To be able to navigate skilfully in a difficult conversation, we must realise that we only see, know, and understand a small part of what is going on. In an earlier chapter we used the systems iceberg model to explore the underlying structures of a complex system. The metaphor of an iceberg can be equally useful when trying to understand the many layers of a conflict.

When we see an iceberg, only a small part is visible above the surface of the water. We can think of this part as the facts of a difficult situation. These are the things we can observe and describe in rational terms. But as we all know, the largest part of an iceberg hides under water. In a conflict, below the surface there are many intangible things such as feelings, expectations, values, and other things that are part of building the tension. When we are facing a difficult situation and want to understand it better, it can be helpful to remember the metaphor of the iceberg and explore three different levels, both from our own as well as the other party's perspective.

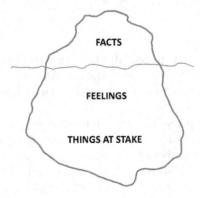

*Figure 4.3* The conflict iceberg.

## Facts

The first level is how we would normally describe the situation if someone asked us to explain it. This level represents our interpretation of the facts, what has happened previously, what is going on, etc. When we are discussing a problem or a conflict, this is normally where we spend most of our time, often arguing about who is right about the facts.

What we tend to forget when we are discussing at the facts level, is that everyone is partially right, but only partially. Typically, everyone involved has some valid point, but no one has the full truth or is totally objective. As we have covered earlier, our interpretation of a situation is always influenced by our own biases and assumptions.

Knowing we do not hold the full and only truth can help us be more open to others' perspectives. This does not mean we cannot disagree on things, but it can help us hold our opinions a bit more lightly.

## Feelings

Below the facts level is the feelings level – all the things happening inside us. Conflicts are per definition never solely rational. Feelings and emotions are triggered which will influence how we interpret the situation, as well as how we think and act.

To navigate a difficult situation skilfully we need to be able to identify and own these feelings. If feelings remain under the surface, unspoken and unmanaged, they will influence the process without us being able to address or work with them.

Recognising feelings in a conflict is not the same thing as endorsing inappropriate behavior. But, by acknowledging that both we and other people involved are influenced by feelings, we can be a bit less judgmental and nurture a more curious and compassionate approach.

## What is as stake

Strong feelings are often triggered when we experience that our values, assumptions, or other foundational aspects of our identity are being challenged. Often this is related to our image of self or how we would like to be perceived by others.

At the root of deep conflicts are often issues related to people not feeling heard or respected for who they are or what is important for them. By being open and curious about what these deeper roots can be, and what is at stake for all people involved, we are better equipped to understand the feelings being triggered and why others see things the way they do.

I invite you to reflect on all the different situations you encounter, bearing these three levels in mind. As we train ourselves to look at conflicts from these three perspectives, we often start to see more nuances to the situations and thereby how we can handle it in more compassionate ways. In the next section, we will look at how we can apply these principles when faced with a challenging situation.

### Approaching a difficult situation using the conflict iceberg

As you can see, the three levels relate to areas we have covered before around biases, emotional patterns, mental models, empathy, etc. Even if we would like to think of ourselves as objective and rational beings, when finding ourselves in a difficult situation we can run the risk of getting so caught up in the situation and our emotions around it that we lose perspective.

The next time you find yourself faced with a challenging situation involving other people, you can try leveraging what we have covered above by reflecting on the situation in three steps:

#### Step 1 – Deepening our self-awareness

Reflect on each of the three levels from your own perspective:

- *How do I interpret the facts of this situation?*
- *What has led me to these conclusions?*
- *Where may I have blind spots or biases?*
- *How do I feel about this situation?*
- *How are my feelings and emotions influencing how I act?*
- *Can I recognise these feelings from other situations?*
- *What are the deeper reasons for me being triggered?*
- *What is really at stake for me here?*

With a good amount of honesty and self-compassion, try to be as open and transparent as possible with yourself. The more you can uncover the different layers of the situation, but better you can navigate in it.

#### Step 2 – Deepening perspective taking and empathy

Now reflect on the same questions from the other party's perspective. Imagine yourself in their situation, how do you think they would answer?

- *How may they interpret the facts of this situation?*
- *What may have led them to these conclusions?*
- *Where may be their blind spots or biases?*
- *How do you think they feel about this situation?*
- *How may their feelings and emotions influence how they act?*

- *Can their reactions be related to other or earlier events?*
- *What may be the deeper reasons for them being triggered?*
- *What could be important things being at stake for them here?*

### Step 3 – decide on how to proceed

Having reflected more deeply on both your own and the other party's perspectives, feelings, and what is at stake, you have a better foundation for choosing an appropriate approach.

Sometimes our self-reflection leads us to see that the root of the issue lies with ourselves, and we can start by working with that. Often our reflection on the other persons' perspectives sparks our curiosity and we realise that we need to do something to learn more. At times, we will find that we need to stand up more firmly for our own point of view, be assertive and have a tough conversation about things where others cross the boundaries for what we think is ok.

No matter how you decide to proceed, the goal of reflecting on the three levels is to bring you to a place where you can act with a higher degree of self-awareness, curiosity, and compassion. This lays the foundation for a going into a difficult conversation, not to win over the other, but with the aspiration to find real and sustainable solutions.

## Leading with a strong back and a soft front

In this chapter on collaborating across divides, we have focused on the importance of cultivating curiosity and openness, to be able to understand the feelings, perspectives and needs of others, and together co-create solutions to complex problems.

However, this emphasis on empathy and perspective taking must not be understood as there is no place for standing up for our own point of view. Earlier we discussed that empathy isn't about giving in to other people, but to understand their feelings and perspectives, while at the same time being able to discern the difference between their needs and yours. Along the same lines, collaborating effectively with people across divides entails being both open and assertive. To act with compassion is not the same thing as giving others what they want, but to act in the interest of a long-term greater good. This can sometimes mean taking a firm stance.

Throughout history, leaders like Mahatma Gandi in India, Nelson Mandela in South Africa, and Dag Hammarskjöld as the Secretary General for the UN, are examples of people who managed to bridge divides and create solutions few thought possible. These leaders were by no means weak. They embraced the paradox between openness and empathy on one hand, and on the other, the courage to communicate and stand up for their vision despite resistance and criticism. To borrow an expression from Roshi Joan Halifax, they lead with a strong back and a soft front.

How to live this paradoxical approach cannot be easily scripted, but below are some examples and metaphors that can guide us and help us get a sense of what it looks and feels like.

### No courage without vulnerability

Brené Brown became world famous through her TED talk on vulnerability, where she shared findings from her many years of research on courage and vulnerability. One of the powerful learnings from her research is that true bravery isn't about toughening up or never being afraid. It is rather about acknowledging our fears and weaknesses and being willing to face them with an open mind.

In her book *Dare to Lead*, Brown shares how she met with Special Forces soldiers who had put their lives on the line many times in real battle. They too confirmed that at the heart of true courage lies the willingness to be with our vulnerability and fears, without pulling out or mentally shutting down.

When we become afraid, it is very easy to put on layers of psychological armor, like showing a tough attitude, distancing ourselves from others and closing down for our empathy. Being vulnerable is to stay with what is difficult without armor and with an open mind and heart. Having a strong back is to dare to step into situations we know will be difficult. Having the soft front is our ability to stay open, vulnerable and compassionate in the midst of it.

Most of us don't have to face armed conflicts or physical threats in our daily lives, but even the ordinary dynamics of organisations provide many situations where we need to show both courage and vulnerability. Especially if we are in a formal leadership role or other position of authority, how we strike this balance will influence the work environment and culture of our organisation.

Striking the balance of leading with a strong back and a soft front is not easy. It invites us to hold paradoxes and explore novel ways to approach our everyday situations. Here are a two questions and paradoxical expressions for you to reflect on:

- If you are a leader, how can you embody an *empathic authority*?
- In difficult situations, how can you act with a *gentle firmness*?

### Being like water

In martial arts, the metaphor of 'being like water' is often used to describe the idea of being both soft and powerful. We can all relate to the powerful forces of the sea or a rapid river. Water can break steel and concrete structures and erode rocks. Yet, water also represents ultimate softness. Water meets obstacles by adapting, finding ways around it or penetrating its pours. The metaphor of 'being like water' is about acknowledging that we can be powerful and influential, while also being adaptive.

The approach of being like water is especially well expressed in the Japanese martial arts form Aikido, often translated as 'the way of the harmonious energy'. Aikido emphasises meeting aggression and resistance with softness. Practitioners train to sense another person's intention and direction of energy. When attacked, the goal is to work <u>with</u> the other person's energy, rather than trying to block it or struggle against it. A skilled Aikido practitioner doesn't back away when attacked but meets the force of an attack with softness and redirects the energy into a throw, lock or other technique that can defuse the situation without adding further aggression.

Maybe the martial arts metaphors seem like a far stretch from your own everyday life but think for a moment of how often we find ourselves in situations where we feel we need to 'defend ourselves'. This is where we can experiment with this principle from the martial arts and see to what degree we can stay composed and feel empowered, and yet be soft and adaptable as we find a way to solve the situation.

### Physical practices to cultivate 'gentle firmness'

Reflecting on and playing with the metaphors above can be a way to find our own understanding of what it means to lead and live with 'a strong back and a soft front'. Another way can be to experiment with how it feels physically.

It is a well-known pedagogical method to engage our body in a learning process and to experience an idea on a physiological level. Below are two practices you can do on your own to get a more embodied experience of finding the balance and integration of forcefulness and softness.

#### Pushing against the wall

In this exercise, we use a physical object to play the metaphorical role of a counterpart.

- *Place yourself in front of a wall, a tree, or any other solid structure, and place a hand on it.*
- *Push on the wall as if you would like to move it. Notice the sensation of pressure and resistance against the wall, and how this generates tension in your arm, shoulders, and body.*

- *Keep your hand touching the wall, but now imagine that it was glowing hot. You are not allowed to lift your hand off the wall, but you still want to have as little contact with it as possible. Notice how this generates a retreating sensation in your body, although your hand hasn't left the surface.*
- *With your hand still touching the wall, shift your approach again to just sensing it. Now you should have no intention to push the wall, but neither do you want to pull away. Your hand just rests gently 'with' the wall. Allow a sensation of the hand and the wall melting together and the boundaries between them dissolving. Notice how this approach of 'being with' the wall feels in your body.*

This short and simple practice invites you to explore, in a physical way, the middle ground between pushing for 'getting things your way' or retreating away from a difficult situation. Having experimented with what this feels like, you can reflect on what everyday situations are where you try to push too much and tense up, or where you hesitate to engage. In what situations would it be helpful for you to apply the middle way where you are 'with' the situation and engage in a firm but gentle way?

### Sitting with a strong back and a soft front

Our physical posture can often mirror how we feel, and we can also influence our own mood and attitude by intentionally adapting our posture. In this sense we can actually cultivate the 'strong back and soft front' attitude in a very literal way by practicing how we sit.

- *Find a place where you can sit comfortably.*
- *Start with taking your seat in a dignified way, placing your hands on your thighs. Ground your feet on the floor and find a position where you feel supported and steady.*
- *Allow your head to float upwards as if someone was pulling a string on the top of your head. Let your back straighten in a way that feels natural.*
- *With your back still straight, allow all the muscles on the front of your body to relax. Notice the softening feeling in your shoulders, chest, and belly.*
- *If you like, you can carefully rock your body back and forth and from side to side, to notice where you have your perfect balance, and the body can be upright without effort.*
- *When you have found a posture that feels balanced and embodies the combination of a strong and straight back and a soft, relaxed front, just stay there for a while.*

- *As you breathe in, imagine strength coming up your spine. As you breathe out, allow the front of your body to soften.*
- *Breathe in a strong back. Breathe out with a soft front.*

It can be interesting to experiment with how our body posture influences our mood. We intuitively know what the body language of a confident versus an insecure person looks like. Conversely, research indicates that deliberately taking a certain posture can also influence our hormones and mental states. Having a straight back and open chest seems to stimulate the release of testosterone which increases our willingness to take risks and face difficulties. Softening muscles on the front of our body stimulates the release of oxytocin, which is a hormone driving empathic behaviors and our sense of connection.

This practice is something you can experiment with on your own, and also bring into your daily work as a 'stealth' practice. Start noticing your own body language and how you sit in different meetings. Try shifting to the strong back / soft front posture every now and then and notice how it makes you feel.

As we have explored in this chapter, collaborating effectively with other people often requires us to find the point of integration where we can be both firm and assertive, and yet open and empathic. There is no easy formula for how to find this integration, but rather something we must continuously explore as we face different situations in life. I hope the principles and practices we have covered will support you in finding effective ways to collaborate with diverse groups of people, also in difficult situations.

## Notes

1 Edgar Schein, *Humble Consulting* (2016), is one of the books where Schein describes the importance and influence of relations.
2 There is a *New York Times* Magazine article that gives an overview of the finding of Project Aristoteles. Search for: *New York Times* Magazine – *What Google Learned from Its Quest to Build the Perfect Team*.
3 Amy Edmondson, *The Fearless Organization: Creating Psychological Safety in the Workplace for Learning, Innovation, and Growth* (2018).
4 E. Thompson, 2001, Empathy and consciousness. *Journal of Consciousness Studies*, 8, 1–32.
5 C. Lamm, J. Decety and T. Singer (2011). Meta-analytic evidence for common and distinct neural networks associated with directly experienced pain and empathy for pain. *NeuroImage*, 54(3), 2492–2502. doi: 10.1016/j.neuroimage.2010.10.014.
6 J. Decety and C. Lamm, 2006. Human empathy through the lens of social neuroscience. *Scientific World Journal*, 6, 1146–1163. doi: 10.1100/tsw.2006.221.
7 The specific experiment is explained in a short video. Search for: *The Brain with David Eagleman – In-Group/Out-Group*. You can find more about David Eagleman's work on his homepage eagleman.com.

 8  Arbinger Institute, *The Anatomy of Peace: Resolving the Heart of Conflict* (2006).

 9  There are articles by Emma Stenström that give more background on the method and the thinking behind it. Search for: *HHS – Bubble Hopping*.

10  xplane.com/worksheet/empathy-map-worksheet. Here you can also find short guide: gamestorming.com/empathy-map.

11  O.M. Klimecki et al. 2013, Functional neural plasticity and associated changes in positive affect after compassion training, Cerebral Cortex, volume 23, issue 7. pubmed.ncbi.nlm.nih.gov/22661409/.
    Participating in Tania Singer's studies has also been Matthieu Ricard, who has a Ph.D in cell genetics, but has spent most of his life as a Buddhist monk. With his experience from both research and decades of deep practice with compassion meditation, he has helped Singer, Klimecki and other scientists explore and understand the differences between empathy and compassion on both an experiential and neurological level. You can hear him elaborate on this in a short video. Search for: *The Difference between Empathy and Compassion by Matthieu Ricard*.

12  On Brené Brown's homepage you can find links to many resources like podcasts with leading thinkers in leadership, articles and more brenebrown.com. She has a relaxed and humorous style, also when discussing deep topics. Her TED Talk on vulnerability is one of the most watched in the world, currently with over 60 million views. Search for: *The power of vulnerability | Brené Brown | TED*.

13  Brené Brown, *Dare to Lead* (2018).

14  You can read more about the various initiatives of Harvard Negotiation Project on pon.harvard.edu/category/research_projects/harvard-negotiation-project.

15  Douglas Stone, Bruce Patton and Sheila Heen, *Difficult Conversations: How to Discuss What Matters Most* (1999).

# Chapter 5

# Resilience and purpose

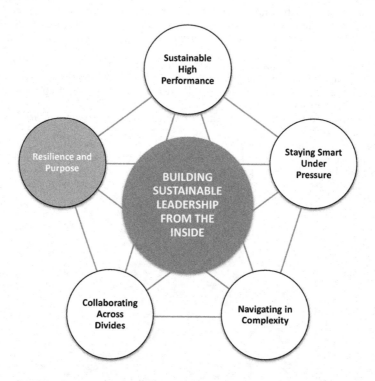

*Figure 5.1* The five areas of building sustainable leadership from the inside.

## Overview Chapter 5: Resilience and purpose

Life will inevitably include both successes, challenges, and setbacks. Based on research in positive psychology, we explore what seems to be the deeper and more sustainable sources of life satisfaction and how we can build a foundation for our personal resilience.

DOI: 10.4324/9781003485148-6

We look at the idea of finding and using an inner compass to guide ourselves through both good times and difficulties, and how our ability to reflect and choose our responses can transform painful events into personal growth.

Finally, we look at the connection between personal development and our responsibility for the impact we have in the world.

*These are some of the areas we are going to cover:*

- Key learnings from positive psychology on what supports well-being and life satisfaction
- Meaning as a source of sustainable joy
- Finding our inner compass and using it to navigate life's challenges
- How choosing our response can shift suffering to learning
- Exploring different building blocks for personal resilience
- The relation between personal development and sustainability transformation
- Connecting to how we are interdependent with others and the world
- Exploring the inner shifts that can lead to outer impact

*Examples of how this part relates to and supports other sections:*

- As we explore resilience in this chapter, we will draw on principles and practices from many areas we have covered in other parts of the book such as self-awareness, emotional regulation, perspective taking and the ability to create meaningful connections.
- The cultivation of empathy, compassion and perspective taking explored in *Collaborating across Divides*, can helps us connect to a bigger picture and find deeply meaningful work.
- Connecting to our inner compass also supports *Sustainable High Performance* as well as our ability for *Navigating in Complexity*.

*Supporting audio material:*
There are guided audio practices accompanying this chapter. Search for *Meditations for Leaders (Joakim Eriksson)* to find them on your preferred audio platform.

In the first part of the book, we explored the topic of Sustainable High Performance and how to find ways to recover and stay clear and calm in a hectic work life. In this final chapter, we will take a wider and more existential perspective on how we can build personal resilience that can help us through the ups and downs in life.

Resilience in this context should not be understood as developing a thick skin or to arm ourselves against whatever life throws at us. As we discussed in previous chapters, approaching life wearing armor just makes us rigid.

There is actually an important difference between being robust and being resilient. The root of the word robust comes from Robur, which is Latin for oak tree. An oak is indeed sturdy, its wood compact and heavy, and its branches very difficult to break. But, with enough pressure from a storm, even an oak tree will eventually break.

Resilience, however, can be likened to bamboo. It is strong but light-weight. Firmly rooted in the ground, but very flexible. When exposed to external forces, bamboo bends with it, but the moment the pressure releases, the bamboo springs back to its original position.

When we are exploring personal resilience in this part of the book, we do it with bamboo as the metaphor rather than the robust oak tree. Our aim is not to be tough and hard, but to be rooted yet flexible. We are going to look at ways we can find our inner compass so we can be intentional and committed to what feels truly important in our life, while also accepting the impermanent nature of the world.

When navigating at sea, it is helpful to lay out a course for where you are heading. But if we encounter difficult weather, we may have to deviate from our planned route. With the help of our compass, we can still find our way toward our destination. Resilience as we will define it here, is about our capacity to apply flexibility and adaptability when circumstances require it, but also use our inner compass to keep moving toward our aspired goals.

## Taking inspiration from positive psychology

Much of what we are covering in this part stems from research in a field called positive psychology. This is not to be mistaken for positive thinking, 'seeing the class as half full', etc. Positive psychology refers to the studies of what makes people thrive and be happy. Interestingly this is a relatively new field of research as much of the first century of studies in psychology focused on mental illnesses.

A leading figure in the field of positive psychology is Professor Martin Seligman[1], who has pioneered research and written multiple books on the topic. In one of his TED talks[2] he shares an interesting overview of three dimensions he and his colleagues have found to influence people's happiness and life satisfaction. There is, of course, a lot of depth and nuances to this field, but below are summarising descriptions of the three dimensions and some key points from studies in positive psychology.

### The pleasant life

This is the dimension of positive emotions, often generated by pleasant, external experiences that make us feel good. This can be things such as enjoying the company of good friends, getting an ice cream on a summer day, buying the car we have been dreaming of, or getting a promotion.

These various forms of positive stimuli and accompanying positive emotions are a quick way to boost our feeling of happiness and life satisfaction. What Seligman's research also shows, however, is that these spikes of positive emotions have a relatively short-lived effect on our overall sense of happiness. Due to what in psychology is called *hedonic adaptation*, we tend to quickly habituate and get used to the stimuli, and the positive effect on our happiness fades away. Studies show that even people who experience major positive events like landing a dream job, or becoming a billionaire, report being back at their previous level of life satisfaction three to six months after the event.

Bottom line: pleasant experiences and positive emotions boost our sense of happiness, but it is not a very sustainable source of lasting happiness. Emotions change, and we typically develop a need for new and bigger stimuli all the time, to generate the same positive experience.

### The good life

The next dimension that influences our life satisfaction relates to what degree we feel that we get to use our strengths and are deeply engaged in what we are doing in our everyday life. When we find ourselves in situations where we are in our sweet spot of competence and have a sense of growth and development, professionally or personally, this brings us a more long-lasting sense of satisfaction, compared to the shorter bursts of happiness triggered by pleasant outer stimuli or a spike of positive emotions.

The area of the *good life* also correlates to what is known as 'flow', first described by Mihaly Csikszentmihaly[3] in the 1970s. The essence of flow theory is about how we find the right balance between the challenges we meet and our current skills and competencies. With too difficult challenges compared to our competencies, we get stressed and anxious. With too little challenge, we get bored. When we strike the balance, we experience a sense of ease and flow while at the same time being productive. In this state of flow, we can feel relaxed while still stretching and developing ourselves.

Seligman's research indicates that when we find flow, engagement and growth in our work and life, this has a more profound and long-lasting effect on our happiness and life satisfaction, compared to the external stimuli of the *pleasant life*.

### The meaningful life

As the name suggests, this dimension relates to doing things that feel deeply meaningful to us. What we see as meaningful can differ a lot between people, from spending our free time training youth soccer teams, to helping homeless people or working as an engineer to develop more sustainable energy solutions. In general, deeply meaningful activities often entail doing good for others or contributing to a purpose that goes beyond one's own individual well-being.

As Seligman's team has followed people's self-reported life satisfaction over many years, the data indicates that spending our life engaged in activities that feel deeply meaningful to us, seems to have the most profound and sustainable effect on our life satisfaction, compared to the other two areas.

The take-away message from this research is that there are different dimensions we can work with to improve our happiness and life satisfaction. This invites us to reflect on if we are striving for the right things. Below are a few questions you can use to explore this deeper. If journaling or flow-writing works for you, feel free to take notes.

- *When do you feel satisfied and fulfilled?*
- *What characterises these moments in your life, and what contributes to the feeling of fulfillment and happiness?*
- *In the realm of the pleasant life, what typically generates positive emotions in you?*
- *What are outer stimuli and circumstances that mean a lot to your well-being and happiness?*
- *What are you currently doing to obtain these things?*
- *From your experience, do these experiences bring you short or more long-lasting experiences of life satisfaction?*
- *In the realm of the good life, what makes you feel inspired and engaged?*
- *When do you experience that you get to use your strengths well?*
- *When do you feel in flow?*
- *What can you do to explore that balance between being comfortable enough not to be stressed and challenged enough to feel that you are growing?*
- *In the realm of meaningful life, what feels deeply important and purposeful to you?*
- *When do you feel that you are contributing to something larger than yourself?*
- *How does that make you feel?*
- *What else could you engage in, that would give you a deep sense of meaning in life?*

There are many ways to live a happy and fulfilled life. One source of life satisfaction does not exclude others and we all need to explore our own way. Research suggests though, that to experience sustainable and long-lasting satisfaction, we should probably find a way to balance our striving for pleasant experiences with also giving priority to personal growth and meaningful contribution. In the following sections, we will look at ways to explore how to find the sweet spot of meaningful work.

## Finding our sweet spot and inner compass

In one of the classical management books of the early 2000s, *From Good to Great*, Jim Collins presented findings of what seemed to characterise companies that had outperformed the market over an extended period of time.[4] One of the characteristics was that these companies had a very clear idea of what their sweet spot was in the intersection between what they were uniquely *good at*, what they were *passionate about*, and what was *in demand* in the marketplace.

By knowing what their sweet spot was and using that as a compass to navigate in the market, these companies seemed to be able to adapt to challenges, innovate and grow better than others in their industry. The same ideas and principles could be applied to ourselves, our career and life.

Over many years I have introduced these principles to leaders in career coaching conversations and had them reflect on the same themes. If you are not already sure what your sweet spot is in your work, try reflecting on these three areas:

### What are you really good at?

If you put your modesty aside for a moment at look clearly at yourself and your track record, you can most likely see some patterns.

- *What are the situations and areas where you tend to perform well?*
- *What are things that come easy to you?*
- *Where do you perform better than many others, even without working hard at it?*

### What are you passionate about?

What we are good at and what we are passionate about aren't necessarily the same thing. This area is about things that feel close to your heart.

- *What is it you love doing just for the sake of it?*

- *If you have some spare time, what activities do you like to engage in?*
- *What are areas of interest that you naturally want to learn more about?*

### What is needed?

This is about exploring what is needed and in demand in the context you live and work. Here you can look at different dimensions like your closest circle of family and friends, the organisation you are working for, the industry you are in, or even the society you are part of.

- *What are challenges that need to be addressed, and problems to be solved?*
- *What competencies and skills are in demand?*
- *What would create value that others would be willing to pay for in a work context?*

I have personally used these three themes over the last decades to reflect on my career choices and where to direct my energy. I have used the questions for flow-writing exercises and kept a page for each of the themes in a notebook, where I have added insights along the way. What has emerged for me over time is greater clarity about where the three areas overlap and I am in my sweet spot. Recognising where my sweet spot is where I can contribute the most has worked as an inner compass for prioritising and setting direction both at work and in life in general.

## Ikigai – the value of living

The idea inspired from Collin's research about finding the sweet spot between what we are good at and how we can contribute, bridges to another interesting idea with roots in Japanese culture.

*Ikigai* is a Japanese expression for that sense of meaning that makes us motivated to get up in the morning. Our Ikigai doesn't have to be related to a grand project but can be about finding joy and meaning in the ordinary things we do every day.

Although the expression is used in everyday language in Japan, ikigai became more widely known as a term after a TED talk by Dan Buettner,[5] where he linked ikigai to so called 'blue zones', i.e. areas in the world where people live much longer than average. Buettner's research had found the Japanese islands of Okinawa to be one of these blue zones and made the connection that the local people's focus on ikigai, finding meaning in life, was part of the explanation of their longevity.

Since then, ikigai has been conceptualised in various ways and you will find different 'models' for ikigai on the internet. But no matter if we believe

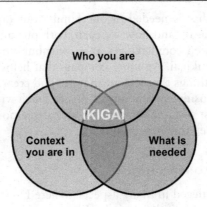

*Figure 5.2* Finding our 'ikigai'.

it can help our longevity or not, finding our own sense of meaning and joy in life can surely be beneficial for our life satisfaction and resilience.

Below is one example of a simple visualisation of what contributes to ikigai, that can be used for the sake of our exploration.

### Who you are

This refers to knowing ourselves deeply in relation to what our values and passions are, as well as our personality preferences and personal strengths.

### Context you are in

Our lives bring us into contact with many different contexts. What arenas are you in touch with, and acting in, at work and in your private life? What is your sphere of influence?

### What is needed

When we pay attention and engage with empathy and compassion, we can see other people's needs and the challenges that need to be addressed. What is needed in the context you are in?

In the overlap between these areas lies what could potentially be our *ikigai*, the way we can contribute to the world we are in and find a sense of meaning even in everyday activities. Finding value in our lives doesn't have to be about doing grandiose things that many people know about. When Mother Theresa was asked how she could accomplish so many great things, she is said to have replied: "I do not do great things. I only do small things with great love".

Reflecting on what is needed in our family, our organisation, or the society we are living in, and how we each, with our unique personalities, set of experiences and competencies, can contribute to that, may lead us toward finding our ikigai. An inner compass that helps us focus our time and energy on the things that feel meaningful and create value. According to the research in positive psychology, being in touch with that meaningful life may be the most sustainable form for life satisfaction, and can keep us motivated, also when things turn difficult.

## From suffering to learning

I see myself as privileged in many aspects. Where I was born, the circumstances I grew up in, that I have my health, etc., give me an easier starting point than many others in the world. I therefore approach this topic with a lot of care and humbleness.

The idea I would like to bring in, however, is that challenging outer circumstances don't necessarily have to determine how we experience the quality of our life. There are many experiences indicating that how we approach difficulties in life, will influence how well we can handle them as well as our sense of agency.

The research in positive psychology points to that our mindsets influence how we look at our possibilities for overcoming obstacles and bouncing back after a setback. What is sometimes called a fixed or negative mindset entail identifying with our mistakes, feeling helpless and believing that a setback will last for a long time. An optimistic or growth mindset indicates that we believe our struggles are temporary and that we have resources to work ourselves out of difficult situations.

Some research indicates that our optimistic or more pessimistic outlook, to a large degree is influenced by genetics. But no matter our genetic disposition, our mindset is also influenced by our mental models and thought patterns, i.e. we can train ourselves toward more of a growth mindset.

As we explored in earlier chapters, by reflecting on and when necessary, challenging our limiting beliefs, we can build our capacity for coping more constructively with difficulties. In that sense painful events can potentially become learning opportunities instead of only causing us suffering.

## The possibility of choice

When faced with challenges, some people like to think there is a higher meaning to why these things happen to them. Whether we have a spiritual or philosophical belief that supports the idea of a higher meaning in life or not, studies show that it helps our psychological well-being to create meaning for ourselves in difficult circumstances.

I would like to return to Victor Frankl here, the Austrian psychiatrist who got imprisoned in a concentration camp during World War II. Being a psychiatrist, he couldn't help noticing how differently his co-prisoners coped with the atrocities and hardships they all experienced. Some prisoners started cooperating with the guards and disclosed things about other prisoners to get personal benefits. Others sacrificed their own benefits to help others.

After his release, Frankl went on to formulate his experiences in a book called *Man's Search for Meaning*,[6] which has been an inspiration for many other authors and thought leaders. Although I used the quote summarising Frankl's message earlier in the book, it is worth repeating here:

*Between stimuli and response, there is a space.*
*In that space lies our freedom to choose our response.*
*In our choice lies the keys to our freedom and happiness*

What Frankl points to is that we cannot rule over the outer circumstances in our life, but we can choose how we respond to them. Frankl argued that in our choice of response we create meaning in our life. When Nelson Mandela walked out of prison after 27 years in a tiny cell at Robben Island, dignified, compassionate, and committed to bring healing to South Africa, he embodied the power of choosing one's response.

To bring this back to our own daily struggles, we can use Frankl's principle of 'choice' to reflect on how we can respond most wisely and skilfully, and how the situations we are facing can help us grow as a person.

### Pain + reflection = growth

Robert Kegan, the developmental psychologist behind the Immunity to Change framework, states that a combination of painful experiences and a person's ability to reflect on them, often leads to personal growth.

Without challenges and setbacks, we are likely to continue life in our habitual ways, with no need to upgrade our mental models or expand our perspectives. If we experience difficulties without the abilities to reflect and process them in a constructive manner, we are likely to suffer more and can easily get caught in blaming, feeling helpless or depressed.

To grow as human beings, we probably don't have to look for pain and difficulties – they tend to show up by themselves every now and then. What we can do, however, is to establish personal habits that make us more able to reflect and cope skilfully with the setbacks when they show up.

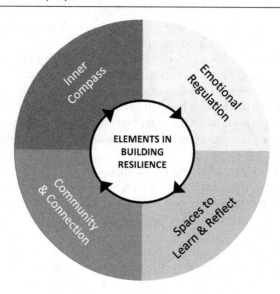

*Figure 5.3* Elements in building resilience.

## Building blocks for resilience

Throughout this book, we have explored a range of personal practices for relating to our emotions, reflecting on our assumptions and mental models, and applying compassion to ourselves and others. To summarise this part on resilience, I would like to offer an overview of four elements, or building blocks, that we all can cultivate to create a stronger foundation for resilience and personal ability to cope with the ebb and flow of possibilities and challenges in life.

The four elements correspond with what research in positive psychology points to as key parts of flourishing and well-being. As you will see, the building blocks also relate to topics we have already covered in different parts of the book. The illustration and explanations just serve to connect the dots and bring the different elements together in the context of resilience.

### Using our inner compass to create meaning and guide our way forward

When we have a clear sense of our sweet spot, what is truly important for us, and how we would like to contribute in the context we are living, we can use that as an inner compass to focus our time and energy on meaningful things. And when challenges throw us off our course, we can more easily find our way back to a meaningful path.

As research has shown, being connected to something meaningful can be a deep source of well-being and can override our frustration when life is less pleasant.

### Developing self-awareness and emotional regulation

Our overall well-being is often more influenced by our mental states than the factual circumstances we are in. By becoming familiar with our mental models and emotional patterns, we can more easily notice when we get carried away, and deliberately choose to pause those emotional autopilots that do not serve us.

Self-awareness and perspective taking allows us to intentionally nurture positive emotions. We can train ourselves to evoke feelings of compassion for ourselves and others, also in the midst of difficult circumstances.

### Creating habits and spaces for reflection

When stressed or challenged, our sympathetic nervous system activates, and we tend to go into tunnel vision, repeating habitual patterns of thinking and acting, often driven by self-protection. To step out of this fear-driven state, we must create spaces where we can reflect and engage our perspective taking, big picture thinking and long-term orientation.

These spaces can be two minutes of mindfulness between difficult meetings, sitting down to flow-write for ten minutes at the end of a hectic work week, or meeting with a trusted friend every now and then to share thoughts and reflect together.

These spaces do not show up by themselves in our calendars, and it is often difficult to find that time when we are in the middle of a challenging period. Laying the foundation for personal resilience is about establishing habits before we really need them. When daily meditation or weekly reflection sessions are already a part of our personal routine, these practices will support us in navigating more skilfully through the various challenges we are facing.

### Cultivating connections and a supportive community

As humans, we are social beings and throughout evolution we have learned to build communities for protection, comfort, and support. Cultivating relations and networks, both at work and in our private life, has proven to be important for both our general life satisfaction as well as our ability to cope with difficulties.

Besides the sense of emotional support we can get from having people around us we can trust and share difficult things with, having a well-established network also increases our possibilities to recruit help and find solutions when we need it.

Like the other aspects of building resilience, cultivating strong relationships is no quick fix. We start by making small investments into this 'relationship bank account', and over time we build a credit we can draw on when we need it.

## Connecting with the bigger picture – personal development in service of a greater good

This book has been focused on building personal skills and capabilities. However, working with personal development shouldn't be approached or interpreted as a narcissistic endeavor, quite the opposite. Building the different inner qualities and capabilities we have explored in this book all aims at making us more able to lead and act in ways that are sustainable, both for ourselves and for the world. I would like to argue that our personal development as individuals is closely linked to the potential for sustainable development in our world at large.

Tackling the wicked problems of our time will surely require structural changes at a macro-level, political action as well as large-scale financial support and incentives. But at the end of the day, all these initiatives will also be influenced by the mental models, emotions, level of empathy, etc., of the people involved. No matter where we find ourselves in different societal or organisational structures, we will all have a role in initiating, driving, implementing, or at least supporting changes that contribute to bringing our world on a good path. Hence, our own levels of self-awareness, compassion, and self-leadership are important components in the transformation toward a sustainable world.

In 2018, a group of thought leaders from academic institutions and non-profit foundations in Europe and the US, together with representatives from a few global companies, sat down to discuss *what it would take to create real momentum behind the 17 Sustainable Development Goals*. The necessary information, technology, and resources were already available in the world to make significant changes, but still progress was slow. A yearly conference was initiated, hosted at Stockholm School of Economics, called *Mind Shift – Growth that Matters*, to bring people from different sectors and industries together to explore this important question.

What grew out of these conferences and the conversations between leaders in various sectors, was an awareness of the need for inner development to enable outer impact. The way we think and relate to the world around us, as individuals and as a collective, enables or creates barriers for positive change. The non-profit *Inner Development Goals*[7] Initiative was founded to research and promote inner development in service of a sustainable future. Since then, the Inner Development Goals Initiative has done several research projects and offer a toolbox[8] of research-based methods and practices which can help individuals and organisations build capabilities to work with sustainability transformations and other complex challenges.

Having been an active part of the Inner Development Goals community for a couple of years, I can recommend visiting the organisation's home page and their YouTube channel.[9] Here you will find videos with thought leaders, elaborating on the relation between inner development and sustainable development, as well as plenty of resources you can use for yourself and the organisation you are working in. This book and the methods and practices I have shared here, are highly in line with the purpose of the Inner Development Goals initiative, and the findings from their research.

## Living in an interconnected world

Our modern, western society is largely driven by an individualistic approach where we highly value our autonomy and freedom to choose our own way of life. This approach has many benefits but can sometimes make us blind to how dependent we are on each other. Today we live in a globally interconnected world where events on other continents can come to influence our own daily life. Being in touch with our interdependence can help us stay humble and consider our responsibilities as global citizens.

Professor Dan Siegel even takes this one step further. In his book *Intraconnected*,[10] he argues that our individualistic understanding of a self, separate and independent from the world around it, is the cause of many of the problems we face in the world. Siegel suggests that by actively exploring how we as individuals are connected with and dependent on other people and the world around us, we naturally expand our perspectives and are more likely to think and act in ways that are beneficial to the whole. Below are two reflection exercises that invite you to do that kind of exploration.

### Reflecting on our breakfast

This is a simple exercise you can do next time you are having breakfast to give you a taste of how interdependent we all are, and how even small, daily habits may have an influence on the lives of others.

- *When you sit down at your table with your food and drinks in front of you, take a moment to notice how many different products and ingredients have been brought together to make your breakfast.*
- *From how many different parts of your country, or the world, have the ingredients been brought to your breakfast table?*

- *How many people have been involved in cultivating, harvesting, trans-porting, and preparing what is now in front of you?*
- *What would your breakfast be like if these people had not contributed the way they do? Before you dig in, extend your gratitude to all these people.*
- *Reflect for a moment on the life conditions of the people involved in making your breakfast possible.*
- *What is the impact your breakfast habits might have on our climate or on other people?*
- *How would it be possible for you to adjust your habits to contribute to the life conditions of others, have less negative impact, and still main-tain your quality of life and have as enjoyable a breakfast?*

### Seven generations from now

This reflection exercise is inspired by Joanna Macy,[11] an environmentalist and author of many books on living sustainably. The original exercise is described in her book *Coming Back to Life*.[12]

Imagine that you are sitting in front of a person who lives seven generations into the future. This person has travelled in time to visit our generation to better understand how we thought and acted in this time.

As you imagine the representative of future generations asking you the questions below, pause for a moment after each question, and reflect on how you would have answered.

- *Dear ancestor, I am so pleased to finally meet you. In my generation we have often discussed how it was to live in your time, and how you thought about things.*

  *We have understood that your generation knew that the well-being of our planet was threatened, and that there were many plans for how to solve it. Still, it seems to have been difficult to act on what you knew. Why is that?*

  ------

- *Now, seven generations into the future, we live on a healthy planet with more thriving societies than in your time. What did you do to change the direction of development?*

  ------

- *We, the future generations, are grateful for your actions. Tell me, how did you find the motivation to change and work for a more sustainable future?*

  ------

This exercise can be through provoking and maybe even a bit uncomfortable. But it just points to what we already know. The way most of us live our lives today is most likely not compatible with a sustainable future, and we, as all generations before us, have a responsibility for what legacy we leave for the future.

### Expanding our circle of concern

By thinking deeply about how we are linked to people around the world as well as how future generations will be influenced by our actions, we might expand our perspectives and sense of responsibility.

In earlier chapters we discussed how our innate capacity for feeling compassion for others often is limited to the people we count as being part of our in-group. To work for a sustainable future in a globalised world, we may have to work on extending that in-group to people in other countries and to future generations who will never meet.

Mother Theresa once said that one of the problems with our societies is that we draw our family circle too small. If we are to find the motivation to change our lifestyles and act on behalf of people on the other side of the planet, or those not yet born, we may need to do the inner work of connecting and feeling compassion for them too.

### Inner shifts for outer impact

Our human brain is the most complex organ known to science and has developed over tens of thousands of generations. Many of our mental functions have been optimised by evolution to support our survival. However, the exponential development of societies and technology over the last century has made some of these functions out of date. In a high-tech and globally interconnected world, some of our more primitive drivers that helped us survive on the savannah, can actually threaten our long-term well-being as a species.

The natural evolutionary development of our brain is a slow process, and it struggles to keep up with the outer development in our modern world. To keep thriving as a human society, we probably need to take deliberate action to speed up the process of upgrading our mental software to match the world we are living in.

So what are upgrades and areas of inner development we can work at to support sustainable development in the world? As we explored earlier, one major thing is probably to expand our circle of concern. To solve the complex challenges of our time, we must be able to think and care about people beyond the smaller in-groups of our specific 'tribe' that our mind naturally identifies with. If we can cultivate understanding and compassion for others across the various mental divides our mind creates, we will be better positioned to collaborate and solve the really wicked issues of our time.

Another theme we need to address is how we pursue happiness. If we are to move toward a fair and sustainable use of resources, we probably need to find alternative paths to life satisfaction than more material comfort and increasing consumption. For anyone who sees these things as the essence of a good life, this can, of course, sound like a dire forecast. This, however, is where the promise of inner development comes into the picture and offers an alternative.

When we start to cultivate deep self-awareness and become more familiar with the workings of our mind, we realise that we can find the sources of a fulfilling life inside us, rather than outside. This doesn't mean we cannot enjoy comfort and pleasurable experiences, but we don't need them as much in order to feel happy. We find freedom in being less dependent on outer stimuli and can shift from chasing pleasures to pursuing deeper meaning in life.

To use terms from the Greek philosophers, we can shift from focusing on hedonia, the pursuit of pleasure, to eudaimonia, the pursuit of deeper fulfilment. With our happiness grounded inside ourselves, we can more easily detach from old habits, make the necessary changes in our lifestyle, and find a way of living that is sustainable both for us, other people, and our planet.

## Who do we choose to be?

In her book, *Who Do We Choose to Be?*[13], renowned systems thinker Margaret Wheatley[14] calls each of us to take leadership, by bringing out the best in ourselves and inviting people around us to do the same. Leadership in this context has nothing to do with formal authority but is about taking responsibility for how we show up and how we contribute in the situations we find ourselves. As Wheatley likes to say: "Don't think too much about if the glass is half full or half empty. Ask yourself – who needs water?".

Stephen Levine dedicated a large part of his life helping people close to their death. He kept being surprised by how many people were so unprepared for the one thing we all know is going to happen. He also realised how easy it is to get caught up in the treadmill of life and not stop to reflect on what is truly important before it is too late.

Levine decided to conduct an experiment on himself, living a year as if it would be his last. In his fascinating book, *A Year to Live*,[15c] he lays out a journey we all can follow where we get to reflect about what is important for us in this life, what relations we need to heal and what legacy we would like to leave. Why wait for dramatic events to wake us up and force us to consider how we want to live our lives?

As Plato said to Socrates; *A life well examined is a life well lived.* When we are intentional and sincere with how we live our life, chances are that we will experience it as more fulfilling, and maybe we will even inspire others to do the same.

May the time-tested principles and practices I have shared in this book be of benefit in your explorations and support you in living life consciously.

## Notes

1 A short bio and many links to Seligman's work: ppc.sas.upenn.edu/people/martin-ep-seligman.

2 In this TED Talk, Seligman briefly explains the three dimensions of a happy life. Search for: *Martin Seligman – The new era of positive psychology – TED*.

3 Mihaly Csikszentmihalyi, *Flow: The Psychology of Optimal Experience* (1990).

4 Jim Collins, *From Good to Great* (2005). You can read more about what Collins calls the Hedgehog Concept by searching for "From Good to Great - Jim Collins Hedgehog Concept".

5 You can find Dan Buettner's TED Talk around Blue Zones by searching for: *Dan Buettner – How to live to be 100 – TED*.

6 Victor E. Frankl, *Man's Search for Meaning* (1959).

7 On innerdevelopmentgoals.org you can find information about the organisation, events, as well as descriptions of the research-based Inner Development Goals (IDG) framework.

In 2023 the IDG become its own foundation, co-founded and supported by institutions like Stockholm Resilience Center at Stockholm University, World Business Council for Sustainable Development, IMD, LUCSUS at Lund University, The New Division, The Human Flourishing Program at Harvard University, 29K and Ekskäret.

8 Here you can find a curated library of methods, practices, etc., that support inner development: idg.tools.

9 Many keynotes, masterclasses and more are uploaded on the IDG Youtube channel: youtube.com/@InnerDevelopmentGoals.

10 Daniel J. Siegel *IntraConnected: MWe (Me + We) as the Integration of Self, Identity, and Belonging* (2022).

11 Joanna Macy has been influential in many areas related to systems thinking and ecological awareness. You can read more about her work here: joannamacy.net, and also learn more about the movement and community around *The Work That Reconnects* here: workthatreconnects.org.

12 Joanna Macy, *Coming Back to Life: The Updated Guide to the Work That Reconnects* (2014).

13 Margaret J. Wheatley, *Who Do We Choose to Be? Facing Reality – Claiming Leadership – Restoring Sanity* (2017). New edition released in 2023.

14 Margaret Wheatley teaches and has written multiple books on topics relating to systems thinking, leadership and organisational development, including the influential *Leadership and the New Science* (1992). She has worked as consultant and senior-level advisor to many organisations worldwide. You can find out more about her and her work here: margaretwheatley.com.

15 Stephen Levine, *A Year to Live* (1997).

# Acknowledgments

My aspiration with this book has been to bridge and synthesise knowledge, experience and wisdom from many different traditions and fields of research. I am therefore standing on the shoulders of many giants, some of which I have referred to throughout the book. It is my sincere hope that what I have shared is a good and helpful representation of their work and that it will inspire many readers to go to these sources and explore them deeper.

Inspiration for this book also comes from many other people I have met throughout the years, who may be less publicly known than the authors I have referred to, but who have contributed to my understanding of what sustainable leadership can entail. These dedicated people range from meditation teachers and martial arts instructors to CEOs, researchers, and academics. There are too many to list, but I want to acknowledge how intraconnected my ideas are with theirs.

Over the years, I have had the privilege to explore and work together with many wonderful colleagues and engaged clients and participants. It is exploring these topics together with them that has led to the principles and practices shared in this book, and I want to express my gratitude for their feedback and support.

Finally, it is the people closest to me who have enabled me to commit to the journey leading to this book. Without the support of good friends and the care and love of my family, this would not be possible. I hope you feel my deep gratitude and love.

# About the author

**Joakim Eriksson** is an experienced leader, facilitator and executive coach with over 30 years of experience with leadership and organisational development. He works with multinational organisations and draws on research and practices from a wide variety of fields such as neuroscience, systems thinking, contemplative traditions as well as his own leadership experience. Joakim lives with his family in the south of Sweden.

For more information, visit www.IQL-Institute.com.

# Index

Note: *Italic* page numbers refer to figures and page numbers followed by "n" denote endnotes.

Printed in the United States
by Baker & Taylor Publisher Services